Advance Praise for *Exodus*
We Are Called to Change the Politics of ___

"David Beckmann is a prophet for our time. I urge everyone who cares about the great problems of hunger and poverty, both globally and domestically, to read this book and to take to heart his call for full engagement in the political process. Beckmann names the issues—the tragedy of endemic poverty—with real clarity and offers hope borne of a confidence that God is in the struggle."

— **Rev. Dr. Michael Kinnamon, General Secretary,**
National Council of Churches USA

"This book is riveting: engaging stories, fascinating statistics, wise strategy, achievable solutions…and hope so rich you can almost taste it!"

— **Dr. Joel C. Hunter, Senior Pastor,**
Northland—A Church Distributed

"I consider it a privilege to endorse David Beckmann's new book. His program for reducing hunger here in our own country and throughout the world is truly worthwhile studying since these are the thoughts of a man who has given his life to such a noble cause."

— **Cardinal Theodore E. McCarrick**

"Beckmann's book comes at a pivotal point in history when a few focused people can reduce hunger and poverty for millions. It is educational, biblical, practical—and, yes, political (in a good way). If you have ever wondered, 'what can just one person do?' here is your answer. It will perhaps surprise you: You can change the world."

— **Sharon E. Watkins, General Minister and President,**
Christian Church (Disciples of Christ)

"Every person who cares about poor and hungry people should read this. It is written with clarity, integrity, and humility. Thanks be to God for David Beckmann and this passionate call to global justice."

— **Daniel Vestal, Executive Coordinator,**
Cooperative Baptist Fellowship

"As followers of Jesus Christ, we have faith that God is at work redeeming the world. David Beckmann reminds us that this redemption includes delivering millions of people from the scourge of debilitating hunger and poverty. One billion people still await deliverance."

— **Rev. Bruce Reyes Chow, Moderator, 218th General**
Assembly, Presbyterian Church (U.S.A.)

"A powerful, prophetic, and deeply personal call to action to end the scandal of hunger in our nation and world. Beckmann charts the road ahead and the policy, political, and spiritual paths we need to take to achieve the moral imperative of 'hunger no more.'"
— **John Carr, Executive Director, Department**
of Justice, Peace, and Human Development,
United States Conference of Catholic Bishops

"Beckmann calls on people of faith to make a difference by encouraging policies that help families escape the ravages of hunger and build lives of self-sufficiency. As we strive daily to live out our calling to love and serve the neighbor, Beckmann's book is a prayer of hope and possibility."
— **Mark S. Hanson, Presiding Bishop,**
Evangelical Lutheran Church in America

"Beckmann offers hugely important insights into the current status of poverty in our world today and efforts to reverse it, and he suggests that God's desire is a new 'exodus from hunger' in which people of faith will play a key role—if we play our part. I strongly recommend this book and the vision it presents."
— **Dr. David P. Gushee, Distinguished University Professor**
of Christian Ethics, and Director, Center for Theology
and Public Life, Mercer University

"Stands as a clarion call for the church to rise above political ideology and prophetically stand on a platform of righteousness and justice in order to deliver the hungry into the hands of hope."
— **Rev. Samuel Rodriguez, President, National Hispanic**
Christian Leadership Conference,
Hispanic National Association of Evangelicals

"Beckmann presents a very compelling vision and strategy to ensure that every citizen of the world has equal access to the most basic of human needs— food. As president of Bread for the World, Beckmann is uniquely positioned to lead this movement of God."
— **Michael Thurman, Pastor, Dexter Avenue**
King Memorial Baptist Church

"Beckmann shows that poverty is not the opposite of wealth but the opposite of justice. Prioritizing legislative policies can not only make justice a reality but can eradicate poverty and hunger in a world of plenty."

—Thomas L. Hoyt Jr., Senior Bishop, Christian
Methodist Episcopal (C.M.E.) Church

"From rural African villages to urban food deserts, everyday miracles are bringing glimpses of the end to hunger and poverty. With a lens for truth, David Beckmann shows that an exodus from the slavery of hunger requires more than local compassion. Solutions are at hand to change the business, the incentives, and the politics of hunger to fulfill God's imagination for shalom in our world."

—Suzii Paynter, Director, Christian Life Commission,
Baptist General Convention of Texas

"The most compelling and convincing call written to date on the hope of ending hunger and poverty. People of faith tend to ignore a huge power they carry with them—the stewardship of their citizenship! Beckmann spells out how this power we carry can break down structures that keep people enslaved in poverty."

—Jo Anne Lyon, General Superintendent,
The Wesleyan Church

"One of David Beckmann's most important contributions to the discussion of overcoming world hunger is his insistence that it is achievable. Here he makes his case based on what has already been accomplished and how such progress can continue. Leaders of faith communities of all sorts can find here a resource for discussion of issues."

—Rev. Dr. Glenn R. Palmberg, President Emeritus,
Evangelical Covenant Church

"Hunger is very personal and has a face and a story. Beckmann brings theology and political action into provocative tension. This book can change our lives both as believers and as citizens. It infuses hope into our dream for a future in which all share in the bounty of creation."

—Christine Vladimiroff, OSB, President,
Conference of Benedictine Prioresses

EXODUS
from HUNGER

We Are Called to Change
the Politics of Hunger

DAVID BECKMANN

WESTMINSTER
JOHN KNOX PRESS
LOUISVILLE • KENTUCKY

First edition
Published by Westminster John Knox Press
Louisville, Kentucky

10 11 12 13 14 15 16 17 18 19—10 9 8 7 6 5 4 3 2 1

Scripture quotations from the New Revised Standard Version of the Bible are copyright © 1989 by the Division of Christian Education of the National Council of the Churches of Christ in the U.S.A. and are used by permission.

Book design by Drew Stevens
Cover design by designpointinc.com
Cover illustration: © Ralf-Finn Hestoft/ CORBIS; © Patrick Laverdant/ istockphoto.com; © Nic Bothma/epa/CORBIS; © Warwick Lister-Kaye/ stockphoto.com; © Marcel Mettelsiefen/epa/CORBIS

Library of Congress Cataloging-in-Publication Data

Beckmann, David M.
 Exodus from hunger : we are called to change the politics of hunger / David Beckmann.
  p. cm.
 Includes bibliographical references (p.) and index.
 ISBN 978-0-664-23684-7 (alk. paper)
 1. Hunger—Religious aspects—Christianity. 2. Church and social problems—United States. 3. Christianity and politics—United States. 4. Economic assistance, American—Citizen participation. I. Title.
  BR115.H86B43 2010
  261.8'326—dc22

                                                                    2010027049

CONTENTS

FOREWORD

Archbishop Desmond Tutu,
Nobel Peace Prize Laureate

I have noticed that many people in the United States think that mass hunger and poverty are immutable facts of life. They may volunteer at a soup kitchen or contribute to an international charity, but do not hope for large-scale change. They are often wary of getting involved in politics.

For most of my life, many people thought that racial oppression was an immutable fact of life in South Africa. As a pastor, I encouraged people who believed in God to get active in pushing for change. In the end, God blessed us with a transition to a more just society.

David Beckmann—a winner of the 2010 World Food Prize—is both a pastor and an economist. He is calling on people of faith and conscience in the United States to get more active in the politics of hunger and poverty. He sees opportunities right now to win changes that would help many people in the United States and around the world escape from hunger.

A stronger U.S. commitment to overcoming global hunger and poverty would be a huge help in Africa and other parts of the world. And you can certainly overcome mass hunger and poverty within the United States itself. Your country is so richly blessed.

David says that God is moving in our time to overcome hunger and poverty and that people of faith in the United States can play an important role in this great exodus. I plead with you to read this book and act on it.

Archbishop Desmond Tutu

INTRODUCTION

I visited an exceptionally poor area of Mozambique in East Africa last year. Our first stop was Mtimbe, a settlement of about forty families on the shore of Lake Nyasa—many miles from the nearest road. They had no electricity or running water, and no shops—just mud houses with thatched roofs.

I was traveling with Dave Miner, a grassroots leader of Bread for the World from Indianapolis who serves as chair of our board. Bread for the World urges the U.S. government to do its part to overcome hunger. I've served as Bread's president for twenty years.

We had flown in a one-engine airplane from the capital of Malawi to a dirt airfield on an island in Lake Nyasa. Waiting for us were Rebecca Vander Meulen, a former Bread for the World policy analyst, and six of her Mozambican colleagues. They have developed what they call Life Teams in the Anglican churches of northern Mozambique to help communities deal with AIDS.

We climbed into a big wooden boat for the trip from the island to Mtimbe. About fifty local people waited for us on shore, singing a praise song, clapping, and moving with the music. The Africans in our boat knew the song and joined in as we neared the shore. Martin, one of Rebecca's colleagues, stood up in the boat as we got close. Smiling eagerly, he shouted out the song and pumped his arms to the rhythm. When the boat touched land, he jumped out to hug his Mtimbe friends.

Our hosts pulled our luggage from the boat and led us toward the settlement, singing and dancing their way up the hill. They carried the luggage on their heads, and Dave and I chuckled to see my big black briefcase, which is usually at home in Washington, DC, making its way up the path on an African woman's head.

The crowd stopped outside Mtimbe's mud-brick church, and Pedro Kumpila, leader of the local Life Team, formally welcomed us. Rebecca thanked the people for their hospitality and then posed a serious question. She asked the crowd to tell these American visitors how they had improved their lives in Mtimbe. People paused as they thought about that question.

Someone expressed gratitude for peace. Mtimbe was repeatedly savaged during Mozambique's sixteen years of civil war. Pedro later told us that he once had to watch soldiers smash a baby in one of the wooden mortars women use to pound cassava. All of Mtimbe's residents had to flee repeatedly to neighboring countries and live as refugees for years at a time.

The woman carrying my briefcase spoke about Mtimbe's school. They didn't have a school ten years ago, but nearly all of Mtimbe's children—even the AIDS orphans—are now learning to read and write.

Pedro noted that people in the community who are infected with HIV and AIDS can now get lifesaving medications. Some neighbors who had been at death's door are taking care of their children, farming, and teaching others about AIDS.

A few people in Mtimbe even have cell phones, which connect with a tower across the lake. Cell phones are a big convenience in a place without roads or motor vehicles.

Mtimbe still faces huge challenges. Each family relies mainly on a little cassava field: if the cassava fails, the family goes hungry. Due to turmoil in the global economy, the prices of corn and rice are high, and the government doesn't have the funds to bring electricity to the provincial capital as planned.

As the sun went down, we met with the entire community. We explained that we were visiting to learn about development in Mtimbe, and the chief and other local leaders introduced themselves. We travelers then retired to Pedro's mud-brick home for supper, which was chicken and a huge lump of gooey cassava. Later in the evening, I struggled to bathe myself in a thatched bathhouse, fumbling with my flashlight and the bucket of water I'd been given. Pedro and his family stayed elsewhere that night so that Dave and I could sleep up off the ground on their wooden beds.

I climbed into the bed and tucked in the mosquito net. As I relaxed and reflected on the past few hours, I was deeply moved by the achievements and hope of the people of Mtimbe. They are among the poorest people on earth, but they are making strides toward a better life.

I was also struck by the U.S. government's impact in this remote place. The U.S. Central Intelligence Agency had a hand in Mozambique's civil war, U.S. ethanol subsidies contribute to high grain prices even in Mtimbe, and Mozambique's government has to delay investment plans because of the financial crisis that started on our Wall Street.

On the other hand, U.S. support for the reduction of Mozambique's debts helped finance schools across the country, including in Mtimbe, and the United States funds most of the AIDS medications in Mozambique. Bread for the World's members in the United States helped the people of Mtimbe by urging the U.S. Congress to support debt relief and development assistance for poor countries.

After visiting several other settlements over the next few days, Rebecca and her colleagues took us back across the lake to the island airstrip. Dave, Rebecca, the pilot, and I climbed into another little airplane.

The plane accelerated up the dirt runway, started to lift off, but then dropped back to the ground. It veered off the airstrip at sixty miles an hour and bounced violently across a field. The plane stirred up large stones, and one smashed the window next to my face. There was a construction site at the end of the runway, and if our plane had traveled straight ahead for one more second, we would have died instantly.

A couple weeks later, on a jet headed back toward Washington, DC, I had another chance to reflect. This brush with death made it very clear to me that I should spend the rest of my life helping spiritually grounded Americans push our government to make a bigger effort to reduce poverty. It is possible to overcome hunger and poverty in our time. The progress that people in Mtimbe have made illustrates this, and if a poor country like Mozambique can reduce hunger and poverty, it's certainly also possible in a relatively wealthy country such as the United States. I'm convinced that the binding constraint is political will, and that stronger leadership from the U.S. government is crucial. I'm also convinced that God is present in this struggle, and that people of faith and conscience should do our part, partly by changing U.S. politics on hunger and poverty issues.

Please don't put this book down without deciding to do something to help build a stronger political constituency for U.S. policies to provide help and opportunity for hungry and poor people.

Progress against Hunger and Poverty

Hundreds of thousands of communities in developing countries have, like Mtimbe, achieved improvements in their lives. The world has made progress against hunger and poverty over the last several decades.

According to the World Bank, the number of people living in extreme poverty in developing countries—those living on less than $1.25 a day—dropped from 1.9 billion in 1980 to 1.4 billion in 2005.[1] The fraction of the population living in extreme poverty dropped from one-half to one-quarter! The global economic crisis of 2008–2009 slowed progress against poverty, but the number of people in poverty is still below 1.4 billion.

Figure 1   **People in Extreme Poverty**

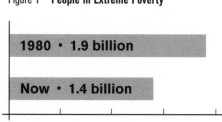

The U.N. Food and Agriculture Organization (FAO) maintains the world's official estimates on undernutrition, and those numbers tell a more complicated story. The number of undernourished people in developing countries declined from nearly 1 billion in 1970 to about 800 million in the mid-1990s.

But the number of undernourished people climbed gradually over the last decade — and then spiked in 2008–2009. Poor people in developing countries typically spend more than two-thirds of their total income on a staple grain such as rice or wheat, so a surge in grain prices caused a spike in hunger. The global economic slowdown also pushed more people into hunger. The estimated number of undernourished people jumped to more than 1 billion in 2009.

Yet that number probably declined in 2010. And even in 2009, the *fraction* of the population in developing countries that was undernourished was less than one-sixth — down from more than one-third in 1970.[2]

Figure 2   **Undernutrition**

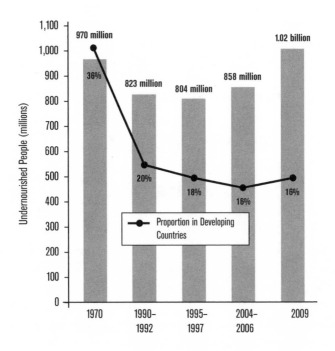

Improvements in health and education have been unambiguous and dramatic. Twenty-six thousand children in developing countries die every day from preventable causes, but that tragic number has dropped from fifty-five thousand daily in 1960.[3] The ongoing carnage is terrible, but the improvement even more remarkable.

Figure 3   **Preventable Child Deaths per Day**

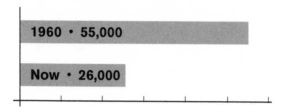

These global trends over recent decades show that dramatic progress against poverty, hunger, and disease is possible. At a U.N. Summit in 2000 all the nations of the world agreed on the Millennium Development Goals to reduce poverty and related ills. The first Millennium Goal is to cut poverty and hunger in half by 2015. Most developing countries are making significant progress on most of the Millennium Development Goals.

Many Americans have come to think that poverty is just a fact of life. They help food banks provide groceries to needy families, but don't expect to see a reduction in the number of hungry people. Experience has shaped these attitudes: in recent decades, our richly blessed nation has not been as successful in reducing hunger and poverty as many other countries.

But the United States dramatically reduced poverty in the 1960s and early 1970s. During those years the United States cut poverty in half. The economy was growing, and unemployment was low. During this period the nation also expanded antipoverty programs. In the mid- to late 1990s, we cut poverty by almost a fourth—again, partly because of government programs.

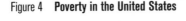

Figure 4   **Poverty in the United States**

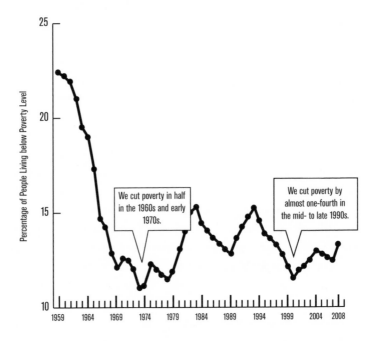

But economic slumps take their toll, and our nation's political commitment to hungry and poor people has fluctuated. Thus, the percentage of people who are living below the poverty line in the United States was about the same in 2008 as in 1970,[4] and recession has since then driven millions more into poverty.

Still, looking back over fifty years, the United States has been able to reduce poverty when the economy was strong and when we made a national effort.

This Is God at Work

I have come to see this generation's struggle against hunger and poverty as a great exodus in our own time. It is like the Lord's deliverance of the Hebrew people from slavery in Egypt on a much larger scale, and God did not send Moses to Pharaoh's court to take up a collection of canned goods and blankets. God sent Moses to Pharaoh with a political challenge: to let Hebrew slaves go free. Moses then led the Hebrew slaves in a great escape across the Red Sea and through a long wilderness journey toward the promised land.

Most spiritually alert people are thoughtful about what God is doing in our individual lives, but often less attentive to God's saving presence in world history. Yet the defining revelation of God in the Old Testament is the exodus from Egypt, and the prophets discerned the presence of God throughout the turbulent history of Israel and Judah. The New Testament then announces that God changed the course of history through the death and resurrection of Jesus and his disciples' mission to the world.

We can recognize God's continuing presence in the world's recent progress against hunger and poverty. When mothers in Central America can't feed their babies, they pray. If they are able to work their way out of hunger so that their children can eat and even go to school, many of these mothers remember to thank God. Those of us who are able to see the scale of progress against hunger and poverty worldwide should thank God for a massive liberation.

As God struggles to overcome hunger and poverty in our generation, God invites us to do our part. We can and should help people in need directly, but one of the most powerful ways to help is also the most neglected: citizen activism.

Why Politics?

Most people keep their distance from politics. All of us are preoccupied with our personal lives. Some people struggle with serious personal problems and really can't devote much attention to public affairs, but more of us just find it easier to focus on ourselves and those closest to us. Many don't bother to pay much attention to what's happening in the wider world.

Americans also tend to have a low opinion of government. We think government programs are inefficient; many people think government is too big and intrusive, and we don't trust politicians. Trust in government usually goes down when the economy is sour, and only 22 percent of Americans now trust the government in Washington. Sixty-six percent of Americans now think that middle-class people get less attention from government than they should; that figure has climbed over the last fifteen years.[5]

Most churches in this country encourage people to help poor people directly and through charities, but say little about changing laws and structures that keep people poor—even though the God of the Bible insists on just laws and is concerned about the behavior of nations as well as individuals.

When I speak in churches, I ask people how they help hungry people. Typically, almost everybody contributes to food charities. Nearly all the religious congregations in the country collect food, maintain food pantries, or support soup kitchens. Some of their members volunteer at food charities. In many congregations, donated food is brought forward to the altar every Sunday morning.

Since the early 1980s the United States has developed a massive system of charitable feeding, and the U.S. religious community has been a driving force. Religious congregations have responded to high unemployment by again expanding their collection of food for people in need. Food banks and food charities now distribute an estimated $5 billion worth of groceries every year. This is a wonderful demonstration of concern, and food charities provide urgently needed help to many people.

But when I ask people in churches whether they have ever contacted an elected official about the national nutrition programs, such as food stamps and school lunches, only a few people raise their hands. Yet all the food provided by all the charities in the country amounts to about 6 percent of the amount of food that poor people receive from federal food programs such as school lunches and food stamps.[6]

In August 2010, Congress passed a bill to provide financial aid to the states. They decided to pay for it partly by cutting $12 billion from future food stamp benefits. That one, quick decision by Congress took away from needy people more food than all the charities in the country can mobilize in two years. But few of the millions of people who contribute to food charities even noticed.

Charitable programs are important to hungry people, but it is impossible to food-bank our way to the end of hunger in America. If we want to make serious progress against hunger, we also need to make our government an active and effective part of the solution.

The national nutrition programs also show that inefficient government programs can be improved. The food stamp program once had a reputation for waste and abuse, but the Clinton and George W. Bush administrations both worked to address those problems. Groups of concerned citizens encouraged the process from outside. The food stamp program, now called the Supplemental Nutrition Assistance Program (SNAP), has become a model of effectiveness. Instead of food stamps, recipients receive a debit card, which makes it easier to track how benefits are spent.

Americans also give generously to charities that work in poor countries. We give more to poor people in developing countries through charitable channels than people in the other industrialized countries (such as Canada, the European nations, and Japan).

But U.S. government programs of development assistance are bigger than all of our international charities combined, and U.S. official development assistance amounts to only two-tenths of 1 percent of our national income — less than the other industrialized countries give.[7] So we're generous in a relatively small way, but less generous when it comes to the most important flow of assistance to developing countries.

People who want to overcome hunger and poverty should definitely support international charities. They work directly with poor communities and help them in ways that official programs cannot. But it's also important to support strong and effective U.S. government assistance to developing countries. The U.S. government can do some things charities cannot do. For example, it can help developing-country governments do a better job in providing public services like schools and rural roads. The U.S. government's decisions and international leadership on trade policies and questions of war and peace also have a big impact on poor people around the world. So in order to achieve the dramatic progress against hunger and poverty that is possible, we must influence how the U.S. government deploys its massive resources and power.

In their pastoral letter *A Place at the Table*, the U.S. Catholic bishops imagined society as a table at which everyone should be welcome and have enough. They described four sets of actors — families and individuals, community organizations and faith-based institutions, the market-place and businesses, and government—as four legs of the table.[8]

We need all four legs to provide a table at which everyone in our country—and around the world—can eat and be satisfied. Progress against hunger and poverty depends mainly on what families and individuals do for themselves. Community organizations and faith-based institutions provide vital, personal help to people who are struggling. What poor and near-poor people most need is good jobs, so well-managed businesses and a strong economy are important. But government policies and programs are also essential, and government is the wobbliest leg of the table. Our government does much less and is less effective than it should be, partly because so many of our citizens fail to do their part in the political process.

The U.S. federal government is especially important, because it establishes the framework within which individuals, charities, businesses, and state and local governments make their contributions. The U.S. government also affects the prospects of hungry and poor people worldwide.

> **The binding constraint on progress against hunger and poverty is political will.**

About This Book

This book is designed to help spiritually grounded people be effective leaders in achieving changes through U.S. politics that would dramatically reduce hunger and poverty in our country and around the world.

The recent setback for millions of hungry people makes this action urgent, and the current political environment makes big changes for the better possible—but only if there is a significant and sustained increase in activism among people of faith and conscience.

Chapters 1–3 discuss the damage that hunger and poverty do, the global recession, the prospect of overcoming hunger and poverty over the coming decades, and what we can learn from countries that have reduced poverty.

Chapter 4 reviews what the Bible teaches about God moving in history with a special concern for poor people. Whatever we believe about God, doing our part to help people in need is crucial to our spiritual integrity. Christians are motivated by the love of God that we experience in Jesus.

Chapter 5 makes the case that a stronger national effort to reduce poverty would be good for the United States. Our nation faces big problems, and getting more serious about justice for poor people would help to maintain the extraordinary security we have long enjoyed.

Chapters 6–7 argue from the experience of Bread for the World and from some encouraging developments in U.S. politics that we have a real chance to get the U.S. government to do more to reduce hunger and poverty. Chapter 8 argues that we are at a pivot point in the history of hunger and poverty, outlines an agenda for policy change, and calls for increased activism among people of faith and conscience.

Chapters 9–11 are about how God has drawn me into this work and how you can get more effectively involved. We need God's help and loving presence.

This book draws together economic analysis, insights from the Bible, and political experience. They are all part of the movement to overcome hunger. I am an economist, a Christian pastor, and an activist, and these pages share what I've learned from all these perspectives.

This book is supported by an interactive Web site, www.exodusfromhunger.org, and I hope you will use it to share your experiences, plans, and ideas. The Web site also provides additional resources, including a study guide for groups who want to read this book together.

In an era of historic possibilities to reduce economic misery, our nation—the world's superpower—can either assume the role of pharaoh or open opportunity to hungry and poor people within its borders and around the world. Throughout history, most superpowers have assumed the role of pharaoh, oblivious to movements of history until the old political order is eventually overthrown. Yet the United States has always had high ideals, and people of faith can rouse our nation to contribute actively to the great exodus from hunger that is under way. Big changes for hungry and poor people depend on committed people across the country—people like you and me. God is calling us to change the politics of hunger.

I want to acknowledge the tens of thousands of people who make up Bread for the World's network: Bread members, activists, donors, church leaders, board, and staff. This book grows out of our experience together as Bread for the World. All the royalties from this book will go to Bread for the World.

I am especially grateful to Eleanor Crook, Pat and Bob Ayres, Terry Meehan, Gerry Haworth, Joe and Mary Martingale, Bob Cahill, Dave and Robin Miner, Barbara Taylor, Jack and Lucy Taylor, Tom White, Malcolm and Lou Street, Paula and George Kalemeris, Carol and Dave Myers, Judy Miller, Tom and Marilyn Donnelly, Nick Zeller, Charles Butt, Jerry and Karen Kolschowsky, Rick Steves, Anne Steves, and Ted Carlson and Catherine

Mouly. These individuals have been among the leading contributors to Bread for the World's work for hungry people over the years.

I'm also grateful to the colleagues who helped me write the book: Jim McDonald, Adlai Amor, Jennifer Coulter-Stapleton, Jamie Thomas, Molly Marsh, Hilary Doran, Steve Hitchcock, Salik Farooqi, Sophie Milam, and Eric Munoz. Thanks, too, to David Dobson and his colleagues at Westminster John Knox Press.

And deep gratitude to my wife, Janet.

PART I

WHERE THINGS STAND NOW

CHAPTER 1

WIDESPREAD AND INCREASED HUNGER

Deborah is a fourteen-year-old girl in Kampala, Uganda, about one thousand miles north of Mozambique. She has a fresh face and sad eyes. On the day I met her, she was wearing a lacy white blouse that seemed brand new, but cheaply made.

Deborah grew up in one of Kampala's slums. When she was a baby, her parents came to Uganda as refugees from violence in Rwanda. Her father became a street beggar, her mother a prostitute. They both died of AIDS. A friend of her father's cared for Deborah for some years, but then he also died.

Deborah now stays with the friend's son. He has abused her sexually. His shack has no door or floor, and he makes Deborah sleep in the dirt across the entryway to help protect against intruders—in effect, using her as a guard dog.

A young woman who runs a children's program let Deborah live with her for a while, and Deborah got a chance to go to school. But years of hunger and neglect were hard to overcome. She was restless and unable to succeed in school.

Deborah sleeps with several men. They give her a meal and a bed. The lacy white blouse was a gift from one of them. Deborah knows that the prevalence of HIV and AIDS in Uganda makes sex very dangerous, but she doesn't always insist on a condom. That puts her on track to an early death.

Deborah is one of the world's 1 billion hungry people, beaten down by undernutrition and many other deprivations.

I live in Alexandria, Virginia, a suburb of Washington, DC—far away from Uganda. One of my sons was once friends with a boy named Jack. Jack was small for his age. Over dinner at our house one night, Jack told me he was worried that he wasn't growing properly. When he and my son decided to get together, Jack always wanted to come to our house, because we had food for snacks.

Jack's parents were immigrants from Portugal. His father had kidney disease and needed dialysis twice a week. Jack's mother was a waitress. She worked part-time jobs at two restaurants. She had managed to get the family into subsidized housing.

She had tried to get food stamps too, but the help her family could get from food stamps was too meager to justify the long waits required at the local food stamp office. I called the office repeatedly, and they didn't answer their phone, presumably because the staff was busy with clients. I did manage to get my church to help with the family's overdue utility bills.

Then Jack's father died, and his mother decided to return to Portugal, leaving Jack behind. Jack moved in with the family of a school friend. It is a large African American family, with more heart than wallet. Last time

I saw Jack, he was working at our local Baskin-Robbins. He had dropped out of high school.

Jack is one of 49 million people in the United States who live in households that sometimes run out of food. He is not as desperately deprived as Deborah, but he has always been poor and sometimes hungry.

The Damage Hunger Does

Hunger kills more young children than any disease. One child dies every three seconds in developing countries, and undernutrition contributes to at least a third of these deaths. Little children are weakened by chronic hunger, so they often die of simple maladies such as measles or diarrhea. Many of the undernourished children who survive never realize their physical or intellectual potential.[1]

Hunger hurts adults, too. Undernourished adults lack energy and are less productive than they could be.

The usual measure of hunger in developing countries is undernutrition. Undernourished people do not get enough food to provide their bodies with the calories they need. They certainly can't afford a diet that would give them the vitamins and minerals that would keep them healthy.

Undernourished families suffer other deprivations of extreme poverty. They drink water from unsanitary sources. Their bodies are weakened by untreated disease. They don't know how to write or add, which makes planning ahead and smart farming difficult. They live in huts that don't fully protect them from the elements.

Women and girls typically suffer most. They have the least education. They work long hours. They walk miles each day with heavy loads of water and firewood. In many cultures they wait to eat until after the men and boys have had their fill.

Of the 1.4 billion people in the world in extreme poverty, almost three-fourths live in Asia (mainly in South Asia, Indonesia, and China). Another fourth live in Africa, and the rest are scattered across other developing countries.[2] African poverty has received a lot of international attention, because most of Africa's people are poor, and for several decades nearly all of Africa was sinking deeper into poverty.

I worked for the World Bank before coming to Bread for the World. The World Bank is an intergovernmental organization that finances development projects and provides policy analysis to developing countries. I helped get the Bank more interested in listening to poor people. A colleague there, Deepa Narayan, initiated a major program of listening to the poor. Her first study, *Voices of the Poor*, was based on interviews with forty-one thousand poor people in fifty developing countries. Poor people everywhere talked about hunger as a defining characteristic of poverty. Many poor people also talked about powerlessness and violence in their lives. Poor women are more likely to suffer wife beating. Poor people are manipulated and defrauded by businesses, government officials, and even people who run charities. They are vulnerable to thieves and thugs, and they don't trust police. Poor people are also more likely to suffer from large-scale violence, since poor countries are more prone to civil war.[3]

Deepa's second study, *Moving Out of Poverty*, based on another massive round of conversations in developing countries, stresses the entrepreneurship and optimism of poor people. A young girl in West Bengal spoke for many when she said, "I can perform any work if I try." Many people climb out of poverty, and the many others who are driven into poverty (often by illness) typically express determination to recover. "If you fall ten times, you have to stand up ten times," said Graciela, a fifty-three-year-old refugee in Colombia.[4]

In the United States, hunger and poverty are not as severe as in poor parts of the globe, but they are still scandalously widespread and damaging. A longtime Bread for the World staff member, Barbara Howell, helped convince the U.S. government to start measuring hunger in this country. The Census Bureau now conducts annual surveys, and the U.S. Department of Agriculture (USDA) analyzes the data.

A total of 49 million people live in households that are food insecure. The USDA divides them into two categories: "very low food security" and "low food security." About 17 million people live in households that suffer very low food security. Their eating patterns are regularly disrupted because they don't have enough money for food. They cut portion sizes and skip meals, sometimes going a day or more without eating. Until 2006 the government rightly called this "hunger." But some officials wanted more precise and less emotive terminology, so they now call it "very low food security."

Another 32 million live in households that suffer "low food security." These families struggle to put food on the table. They usually find ways to make ends meet, but sometimes have to skip meals or reduce portion sizes.[5]

A common pattern among food-insecure households is that the family runs out of food before the end of the month. SNAP benefits (food stamps) are renewed at the beginning of the month, and SNAP benefits are not enough to pay for food for the entire month. Some workers also get wage checks at the start of the month. As food runs low toward the end of the month, the mother typically stops eating properly first in order to protect her children. During the last days of the month, the children also have to skip meals. They go to school in the morning with no breakfast and may also go to bed hungry.

Obesity has also become a big problem in the United States. Two-thirds of adults and one-sixth of children are now overweight or obese. Obesity is a problem among all income groups, but food insecurity contributes to obesity among low-income people. Food-insecure families eat cheap food rather than good food, and food that is high in fat and calories tends to be less expensive.[6] An especially high rate of obesity among some groups of poor women may be linked to the fact that they periodically go without food so that their children can eat. When SNAP benefits or the paycheck arrives, these mothers may overeat to make up for days of not eating.[7]

Food insecurity does its worst damage to children. When the body doesn't get enough nutrition, the brain isn't fully alert. Children are designed to be learning machines, but a preschool child in a food-insecure family cannot be as curious as God means her to be. Schoolchildren who aren't getting enough to eat can't concentrate. They fidget and misbehave. The intellectual and personal development of children in chronically food-insecure households is likely to be permanently stunted. As they grow into teenagers and adults, they are more likely to have problems with addiction, drop out of school, have babies out of wedlock, and get in trouble with the law.

Nearly one in four children in the United States—22.5 percent as of December 2008—lives in a food-insecure household.[8] God, forgive us.

The statistical connections between food deprivation, health problems, and how well children do in school are well documented. Dr. Larry Brown at Harvard University estimates that widespread hunger in the United States costs our society at least $90 billion a year.[9]

While most of the people who are food insecure are white, more than a quarter of African Americans and Hispanics live in food-insecure households.[10] Hungry people live in every city and state in the country, with especially high rates of hunger in pockets of poverty such as the Mississippi River Delta and Native American reservations.

U.S. hunger is interconnected with poverty and related social ills: unemployment and low wages, lack of education, inadequate health care, racial discrimination, the strains on marriage in our society, substance abuse, crime, violence, high rates of imprisonment, and homelessness. Actions to address these problems also reduce hunger, and tackling hunger helps to resolve these other problems.

Children in single-parent families are much more likely to be poor, and the number of children in single-parent families has skyrocketed since the 1970s.[11] Whatever we can do to reduce the number of children born outside marriage, as well as the divorce rate, will help reduce childhood hunger. At the same time, policies that boost the incomes of poor and near-poor parents will reduce the exceptional stress on their marriages.[12]

The best, most durable way to reduce hunger and poverty is employment. A good job puts food on the table, includes health insurance for the family, and allows for savings and educational opportunities that can make the family secure. When hungry and poor people are asked what would help them most, they almost always talk about employment, wages, or training that would allow them to earn more money.

Most Americans are vulnerable to poverty. Many people live paycheck to paycheck, so an illness or divorce can be financial disaster. Economist Rebecca Blank studied poverty over a thirteen-year period; she found that one-tenth of all Americans were poor during most of that time, but one-third of all Americans were poor for at least a year.[13] Nearly two-thirds of Americans qualify for one of the government programs that help low-income people at some point in their lives.[14]

Economic Turmoil Has Increased Poverty

The global economy delivered a harsh blow to hundreds of millions of very poor people even before the U.S. financial system went into crisis. The prices of the basic grains on which poor people in developing countries depend— rice, wheat, corn, or sorghum—doubled between 2006 and 2008. Prices have come down since then, but they still remain higher than before.

Grain prices are expected to stay high.[15] The many people in China, India, and other developing countries who have escaped from hunger over the last couple of decades are eating more and eating some meat. This is wonderful, but it puts upward pressure on prices. In addition, the promotion of biofuels in the United States and other countries diverts some land use from producing food to producing fuel.

The global financial crisis and global economic slowdown have also caused hardship around the world. Developing countries have lost exports and investments, and migrants to richer countries no longer have as much money to send home. These economic problems have added to hunger and poverty.

In this country, high food and fuel prices combined with the mortgage crisis, tight credit, and high unemployment to increase hunger and poverty.

Mortgage problems among borrowers who were only marginally creditworthy triggered the Wall Street crisis of late 2008. A 2007 Bread for the World Institute report focused on exploitative financial practices in low-income communities, including the promotion of subprime mortgages to families for whom they could spell disaster.[16] But we didn't anticipate the risk that exploitative lending posed to the whole financial system. Wall Street institutions bought up risky mortgages and repackaged them in complicated ways. As the vulnerability of huge investment houses such as Lehman Brothers became clear, consumers and businesses in the United States and worldwide lost confidence in the economy. We all cut back on spending, and the global economy contracted.

Millions of people lost their jobs, and finding a job became much more difficult. During a past recession, President Ronald Reagan spoke eloquently — from his own family's experience — about the pain of unemployment:

> To me, there is no greater tragedy than a breadwinner willing to work, with a job skill but unable to find a market for that job skill. Back in the dark days of the Depression I saw my father on a Christmas Eve open what he thought was a Christmas greeting from his boss. Instead, it was a blue slip telling him he no longer had a job. The memory of him sitting there holding that slip of paper and then saying in a half whisper, "That's quite a Christmas present," it will stay with me as long as I live.[17]

Recently I preached at a social-justice revival among African American churches in Martinsville, Virginia. This southern Virginia town was a center of textile and furniture manufacturing, but most of its factories closed in the face of competition from developing countries. The recent recession pushed unemployment even higher — to

20 percent. Our revival service was jubilant. But before church I talked with two well-dressed middle-aged men who have endured years of unemployment. Both have searched for jobs throughout the region and gone back to the community college to develop new skills, but without success.

What Will Recovery Bring?

The global economy now connects everything to everything, and today's multifaceted economic malfunction is likely to trigger more problems we can't anticipate. But I am optimistic about economic recovery, mainly because the peoples and nations of the world have a record of resilience in tough economic times.

I am also encouraged by the way the United States and other governments have responded to the crisis. President George W. Bush's bank-recovery program in 2008 kept the financial crisis from spinning out of control, and President Barack Obama followed with a massive stimulus bill in 2009.

Half of the $850 billion in President Obama's stimulus bill went to programs that include low-income people. When Bread for the World's analysts first reported this, I asked them to check their figures. The news seemed too good to be true. But focusing on low-income people made sense, because they most needed help. Also, low-income people spend nearly all the money they get, so help for low-income people quickly boosts the rest of the economy.

President Obama was also right to use some of the stimulus funding for initiatives to make the U.S. economy more environmentally sustainable—programs to weatherize schools and low-income housing, for example. Climate change is real, and a recovery that ignores environmental constraints will not be long-lasting.

The United States won't recover to the society we were before this economic crisis. We will recover to something different, and we can use this crisis to decide what kind of nation we want to be. Many families have reacted to financial constraints by deemphasizing consumption and putting more emphasis on the things money can't buy. At the same time, about half of U.S. voters say the economic crisis has made them more supportive of policies and programs to help hungry and poor people.[18]

We just might achieve lasting cultural changes for the better, just as the generation that endured the Great Depression learned lifelong lessons about hard work, frugality, compassion, and the value of government social programs.

CHAPTER 2

DRAMATIC PROGRESS
IS FEASIBLE

*God, grant me the serenity to accept the things I cannot change, cour-
age to change the things I can, and the wisdom to know the difference.*
—*Reinhold Niebuhr*

Most people think world hunger is absolutely hope-
less, something we cannot change. Trying to end
world hunger seems quixotic, almost a joke. But dramatic
progress against hunger and poverty is possible.

I don't think we can do away with *all* hunger. Some
addicts, for example, will be so consumed with their
addiction that they will fail to secure food for themselves.
Globally there will continue to be outbreaks of hunger in
countries that are oppressed by war or tyrants.

But we do not have to accept the intermittent hunger
of 49 million people who live in food-insecure families in
the United States. Once the economy is growing again, it
is feasible to drive down the extent of hunger in America
to, say, 5 million people. Developing countries that are at

peace and have decent governments can also dramatically reduce hunger. Some developing countries have reduced both hunger and poverty, and it's easier to reduce hunger than poverty, because food assistance programs can end hunger among families that are still poor. Within several decades, we can reduce the number of undernourished people in the world from 1 billion people to, say, 100 million, ending the routine mass hunger that has plagued humanity throughout history.

Hurrah for the Millennium Development Goals!

In the 1990s Bread for the World Institute tried to figure out what it would take to end hunger. Many people and institutions around the world were thinking along the same lines.

A series of U.N. conferences in the 1990s set global goals for the environment, hunger, population, and other issues. By the end of the decade, the development assistance agencies of industrialized countries wanted to boil these agreements down into a manageable set of goals, with quantitative indicators by which they could monitor progress. These goals were embraced by the heads of government of the eight most powerful countries in the world at their annual Group of 8 (G8) Summit.

At the United Nations, the developing countries also embraced these goals. They added some specifics about what the industrialized countries should do to help, and virtually all the nations of the world approved them in 2000 as the Millennium Development Goals.[1] Presidents George W. Bush and Barack Obama have both affirmed that the United States will do its part to achieve these historic goals.

THE MILLENNIUM DEVELOPMENT GOALS

1. Eradicate extreme poverty and hunger
2. Achieve universal primary education
3. Promote gender equality and empower women
4. Reduce child mortality
5. Improve maternal health
6. Combat HIV/AIDS, malaria, and other diseases
7. Ensure environmental sustainability
8. Develop a global partnership for development

The Millennium Goals articulate aspirations that people around the world now share. Virtually all the world's religions and competing ideologies affirm efforts to overcome hunger, extreme poverty, and related ills. Many governments and people around the world are now using the Millennium Goals to guide and measure their work. Bread for the World focuses on hunger, but we understand that hunger is interconnected with the other aspects of poverty, so we have embraced the Millennium Goals as the framework for our international advocacy.

When the Millennium Development Goals are described to Americans, about half of us find them inspiring. The other half find the idea of a comprehensive, internationally agreed strategy to reduce poverty utopian. But if you ask about specific goals—letting all the world's children go to school, for example—nearly all Americans are supportive.[2]

The Millennium Goals helped inspire the industrialized countries to more than double the amount of their total development assistance from $53 billion in 2000 to $121 billion in 2008.[3] The donor countries have also agreed, at least in theory, on strategies to improve the quality of development assistance.[4] Many developing-country governments are using the goals to track development progress, and some have focused additional resources on achieving the goals.

The United Nations has done a good job promoting the Millennium Goals and monitoring how the world is doing in relation to the quantitative targets. I served on the Hunger Task Force for the U.N. Millennium Development Goals Project, led by Jeffrey Sachs, one of the world's leading economists. The project developed strategies for achieving the goals, including estimates of what it would cost and how much of the cost could be borne by poor countries themselves. Sachs concluded in 2005 that annual development assistance from the industrialized countries would need to increase by roughly $70 billion right away, with the increase rising to $130 billion by 2015.[5] If the United States would provide a fourth of $130 billion (which is sometimes considered our fair share for joint projects among the industrialized countries), the U.S. share of the cost would be roughly $33 billion.

More development assistance will not, by itself, cut world poverty in half and achieve the other Millennium Goals. Hundreds of millions of poor people must—and will—work hard over many years. Corrupt governments need to be reformed or replaced. The quality of development assistance and trade policies needs to improve. But the $33 billion figure gives us a rough idea of how much it would cost the United States to do its share to achieve the Millennium Development Goals.

Most developing countries are not on track to meet all the goals. Progress has lagged far behind targets in some of the poorest countries and for some of the goals—notably, maternal health and sanitation. Yet the accomplishments for the developing countries as a whole are striking:

— The proportion of children under five years old who are underweight declined by one-fifth between 1990 and 2005.
— Enrollment in primary school increased from 80 percent in 1991 to 88 percent in 2006. Much of this increase is because girls are now going to school, too.
— The number of deaths from AIDS fell from 2.2 million in 2005 to 2 million in 2007, and the number of people newly infected declined from 3 million in 2001 to 2.7 million in 2007.
— Deaths from measles dropped by two-thirds between 2000 and 2006. The incidence of tuberculosis has stabilized or begun to fall in most regions. Malaria prevention is expanding rapidly.
— 1.6 billion people have gained access to safe drinking water since 2001.[6]

The gap between rich and poor in the world is extreme: the richest 10 percent of the world's people receive roughly one-half of total world income, while the poorest 10 percent receive less than 1 percent. It is not clear whether the global distribution of income is becoming more or less unequal.[7] But if the pace of progress against extreme poverty that was maintained between 1990 and 2005 can be achieved for the decade between 2005 and 2015, the world will cut extreme poverty in half between 1990 and 2015.

That last sentence bears repeating: If the pace of progress against extreme poverty that was maintained between 1990 and 2005 can be achieved for the decade between 2005 and 2015, the world will cut extreme poverty in half between 1990 and 2015.

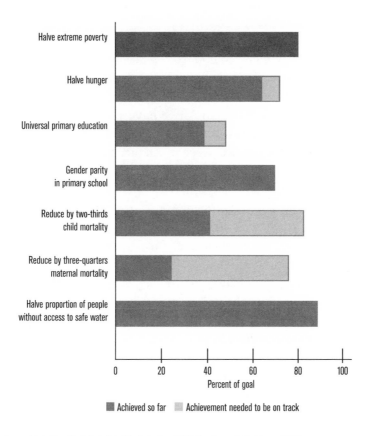

Figure 5 **Progress toward the Millennium Development Goals**

Percent of goal

■ Achieved so far ■ Achievement needed to be on track

Source: Adapted from World Bank, Global Monitoring Report 2010. Based on available data as of 2009.

Good News from the Developing World

In the 1990s the two most discouraging themes in international development were Africa and AIDS. Nearly all African countries had suffered decades of economic decline, and AIDS was completely out of control, killing off much of a generation in some countries.

But much of Africa has since then made huge changes for the better. Most notably, 29 million more African children are in school today than in the year 2000.

Steve Radelet, development advisor to Secretary of State Hillary Clinton, is finishing a book on Africa which is titled, aptly, *Emerging Africa: The Unheralded Development Turnaround in (Half of) Africa*. Steve notes that seventeen countries in sub-Saharan Africa have since 1995 increased the average income of their people by 50 percent and reduced poverty by 20 percent. All but three of these countries have also become democracies.[8]

The world has also fought back against AIDS. Few HIV and AIDS patients in developing countries had access to AIDS medication in the 1990s. Now 3 million patients are on antiretroviral medication.[9] Nearly all of them are living normal, productive lives. The availability of medication has also encouraged people to seek testing for HIV, thus helping to reduce the disease's spread.

Many developing countries have also managed to put dictatorship and war behind them. The number of developing countries holding elections increased from 91 in 1991 to 121 in 2008.[10] The end of the Cold War and increased peacemaking efforts by the United Nations have reduced the number of wars in developing countries over the past thirty years.[11]

Radios and cell phones are now widespread in poor countries. Two hundred million Africans have cell phones, and that number is growing by 60 million a year. Isolated farm families use them to learn about farm prices at market and to contact family members working in the city, and improved communication is also helping to make governments more accountable.

I once asked a former minister of agriculture in Uganda why her government had been responsive to the people even before the formal transition to democracy. She noted that Uganda now has fifty radio stations that broadcast music and news in many languages. When she was interviewed on radio, farmers would call from remote parts of Uganda to let her know if her programs weren't working well in their areas.

The 2010 earthquake in Haiti again brought images of extreme suffering into our living rooms. Haiti faces exceptional challenges—a long history of exploitation by foreign powers, class conflicts, corruption, and now a massive reconstruction task. Yet the number of deaths due to routine poverty around the world is equivalent to a Haitian earthquake every week, and the ongoing poverty of Bangladesh or Tanzania seldom shows up on our television screens. All the good news that is coming from countries like Bangladesh and Tanzania almost never shows up on our television screens.

JEROME SARKAR

When I think about hopeful trends in developing countries, I think of my friend Jerome Sarkar. My wife Janet and I spent most evenings with him when we were working in northwest Bangladesh many years ago. Jerome was my colleague on the staff of the Rangpur Dinajpur Rural Service, a grassroots development agency that Lutheran churches around the world support.

Bangladesh had just been through its war of independence from Pakistan. The U.S. secretary of state at the time, Henry Kissinger, predicted that Bangladesh would always be an "international basket case." But the proportion of Bangladesh's population in poverty has dropped since its independence from 70 percent to 40 percent. Literacy has more than doubled, and child mortality is less than half of what it was. Bangladesh has maintained economic growth and democracy since the early 1990s.[12]

Jerome kindly sent me his thoughts on how his own life has intertwined with his nation's progress against poverty.

In 1945 my father fell seriously ill and died at the age of thirty-eight. Our mother with her five children was at a loss. Nothing could save us without intervention of Almighty God and we were praying to Him for His mercy. An American priest, Father Norkauer, appeared as God's angel and arranged to put us in an orphanage.

His sister later funded my education at Holy Cross High School. The priests who ran the school also helped poor people from time to time with food, medicines, and money. This made a big impression on me.

I took a position in a pharmaceutical company and completed my bachelor's degree attending a local college on the night shift. I then married my wife Maria and started family life.

In the early seventies, Bangladesh was in political turmoil. At the beginning of the liberation war, we had to flee and take shelter in a village. Due to lack of law and order, common men like us were passing our days in helpless conditions. The company where I was working also suffered a setback in business. During the postwar turmoil, nepotism and corruption were the rule of the day. Because of abuses within my company, I decided to leave.

Through a friend, I approached the director of Rangpur Dinajpur Rural Service (RDRS) and joined the organization in 1975. I helped to manage a grassroots construction program in northern Bangladesh. If villages would provide labor and local materials, RDRS would help them build a school or a culvert for a local road. Besides fulfilling my official responsibilities, I helped RDRS staff members form a cooperative credit union for their own self-advancement. I eventually moved to the RDRS office in Dhaka and then retired from full-time service in 1995.

My wife Maria left this earthly abode for eternity in 1993. Maria and I were blessed with four children. My youngest son Hubert died while doing his master's in structural engineering. My eldest son, a master's in economics, is serving in a commercial bank as an executive. My second son, a master's in statistics, is a professor in a leading college, and my daughter, a bachelor's in arts and education, is a teacher in a school. My daughters-in-law are also master's degree holders. In a country like Bangladesh, I have enough ground to be happy.

I started my life in poverty and now, though not a moneyed man, I am contented. I have been enriched by life's experiences through thick and thin. Faith in my Creator, courage to accept help from friends, and a growing sense of responsibility toward others have led me to meaningful living and satisfaction.

Looking back, I offer these observations:
a. Poverty is not a curse. Poverty brings us closer to Almighty God. Bangladesh is home to millions of poor people, and the poor know that God is with them. Who else do they need?
b. Friendship between the wealthy and the poor can benefit both. The wealthy can help the less fortunate better their living condition and, in the process, find meaning as a worker in God's plan.
c. Bangladesh was known by the whole world as the poorest of the poor. Despite many flaws even today, Bangladesh has made tremendous strides toward development over the years.
d. The United States was always considered the most powerful and wealthy nation. Americans always had their say about the poverty, backwardness, and human rights conditions in other countries. Nobody ever dared

to talk about them. Interestingly, today, even in Bangladesh, conscious groups talk about poverty in America, human rights violation by Americans, and underdevelopment in certain sections of the American community. Yet the process of introspection has started, and some Americans are taking steps to veer the ship to the right direction for the U.S.A. and the globe at large.

The United States Can Reduce Poverty . . . When We Try

Poverty in the United States is not nearly as severe as poverty in Bangladesh. Most poor Americans have amenities that would qualify them as middle class or better in Bangladesh: running hot and cold water, a toilet and shower, a television, a telephone, and access to public roads, schools, and hospitals. Yet poor people in the United States suffer hunger, disease, economic anxiety, indignity, poor schooling, and violence.

The United States used to be a powerful poverty-reduction machine. My own great-grandparents homesteaded in Nebraska. They and their children lived simple lives and sometimes suffered deprivation, but they worked hard and prospered. My parents' generation went through the Depression and worked sacrificially to get ahead. I grew up surrounded by comforts and opportunities that my grandparents couldn't have imagined.

Most American families have experienced similar improvements in living standards. In 1900, about 40 percent of all Americans were poor. That declined to 25 percent in the mid-1950s.[13] The poverty rate declined further in the 1960s and early 1970s, and has fluctuated between 11 and 14 percent since 1973.

Economic growth drove most of the nation's past progress against poverty, but government programs also helped. The Homestead Act gave my great-grandparents their farmland. The development of public schools and colleges set the stage for my mother and father to improve their lives. The great majority of their generation was able to finish high school, and my father went to college and graduate school at the University of Nebraska, a public land-grant institution.

During the New Deal and the Second World War, government policies and organized labor combined to create a broad middle class. During that period the rich got poorer, while workers got considerably richer.[14] After the Second World War, the GI Bill gave a huge boost to many people.

The historical experience of African Americans and other people of color has been very different. African Americans endured slavery and then legalized segregation and discrimination. Native Americans were forcibly removed from their lands. Racial and ethnic minorities still have to cope with prejudice and discrimination in employment, housing, and social life. They suffer much higher rates of hunger and poverty than the white majority.

The civil rights movement of the 1960s ended many systems of discrimination and gave African Americans the right to vote. The civil rights movement and the Black Power movement of the late 1960s also helped convince the country to expand antipoverty programs during the Johnson and Nixon administrations.

President Johnson's Great Society programs have been much maligned. President Reagan later quipped that "we declared war on poverty, and poverty won." But, in fact, the Great Society programs played an important role in reducing poverty in the 1960s and early 1970s.

President Nixon ended some of Johnson's programs, notably those that helped poor people gain power through publicly funded lawyers and community organizations.[15] But the Nixon administration continued and expanded others. Nixon's expansion of the national nutrition programs, for example, eliminated the kind of malnutrition we now associate with poor countries. A team of doctors supported by the Field Foundation studied hunger in poor parts of the country in the late 1960s and then made return visits ten years later. Their second report noted great strides against hunger:

> In the Mississippi delta, in the coal fields of Appalachia and in coastal South Carolina—where visitors ten years ago could quickly see large numbers of stunted, apathetic children with swollen stomachs and the dull eyes and poorly healing wounds characteristic of malnutrition— such children are not to be seen in such large numbers.[16]

Programs for elderly people that expanded in the 1960s were also maintained. Between 1959 and 1980 the proportion of elderly people in poverty dropped from 35 percent to 16 percent, almost entirely due to Social Security, Medicare, and Medicaid.[17]

Yet, at the same time, the structure of the economy was starting to change in ways that would make it harder for unskilled people to provide for their families. Technology and knowledge were becoming more important in the economy, depressing incomes for workers without much education. In order to guard against inflation, our nation stopped trying to keep unemployment as low as it was in the 1960s. Competition from developing countries also had some negative effect on the wages of low-skilled workers in this country. Finally, the importance of labor unions has declined. These shifts combined to depress the average wage of unskilled workers, which is now a third lower than it was in 1970.[18]

U.S. health and education have continued to improve:[19]

	Life Expectancy (years)	High School Diploma (%)	College Degree (%)
1970	71	55	11
2005	78	85	30

The poverty rate declined again during the Clinton administration. The country enjoyed exceptional peace and prosperity during those years, and President Clinton made a strong economy his priority. He also expanded the Earned Income Tax Credit for low-income workers.

But progress against poverty has not been sustained. The poverty rate has gone up and down over the last several decades, correlated closely with the rate of unemployment. We should not be surprised. Think about our presidents since 1974: Gerald Ford, Jimmy Carter, Ronald Reagan (two terms), George H. W. Bush, Bill Clinton (two terms), George W. Bush (two terms), and Barack Obama. Reducing poverty has not been a top priority for any of these administrations. Other problems and voter concerns have always taken precedence.

I sometimes do interviews with journalists from developing countries, and they are usually bewildered that a country as rich as the United States still puts up with widespread hunger and poverty. Arguably, the kind of poverty that persists in the United States is harder to overcome than mass poverty in developing countries. In poor countries, nearly everybody is poor. The provision of schools, roads, and improved technologies allows the population as a whole to raise its standard of living. In a highly developed country like the United States, the population that remains poor includes a higher proportion of people with physical or mental disabilities. On the other hand, the United States has vastly more resources from which to draw in dealing with these problems. The average income of people in this country is higher than almost any place else in the world, and U.S. economic output per person has more than doubled since 1970.[20]

The U.S. government's data on food insecurity allows us to guesstimate how much it would cost to end food insecurity in the United States. We know from the official data that the extra groceries needed to make all families food secure would cost roughly $34 billion a year (in a time of normal employment). Expanding SNAP or the Special Supplemental Nutrition Program for Women, Infants, and Children (WIC) would not get groceries precisely to the families that need them. But we might use, say, $50 billion as an order-of-magnitude estimate of what it would cost to end food insecurity in the United States through food assistance programs once the economy recovers.

Just providing food to food-insecure households would not be the best way to end food insecurity. It would be better to complement food assistance with initiatives that would help food-insecure families work their way out of poverty. But the $50 billion figure provides a rough sense of what it might cost to end food insecurity in the United States.

The $50 billion guesstimate, together with the $33 billion estimate of what it would cost for the United States to do its part to achieve the Millennium Development Goals, shows that the costs of dramatic progress against hunger and poverty are not prohibitive.

The United States spent $190 billion on the wars in Iraq and Afghanistan in 2008. The Bush tax cuts are costing the United States about $150 billion a year.[21] Americans spend $48 billion a year on food and care for our pets.[22]

As Dr. Martin Luther King Jr. put it in his Nobel Prize lecture, "There is no deficit in human resources; the deficit is in human will."[23]

KAREN JEFFERSON

As I think about the struggle to overcome poverty in this country, I think especially about Karen Jefferson. She served for several years as my executive assistant. Karen wrote about her determined climb from welfare to work in Bread for the World's newsletter.

My story echoes those of many other young single moms who become pregnant and must care for a child with no job, no skills, and no support. I'm sure some people will argue that I could have gotten a job. That's easier said than done when you are in that position. In my situation, welfare was the only sensible option. It was my saving grace in more ways than one.

I am passionate about helping less fortunate people, and having been on welfare has emphatically strengthened the way I feel. The experience humbled me tremendously and put a lot of things in perspective.

I found myself on welfare shortly after graduating from high school, and I was in the system for close to ten years. I had two children while on welfare, one at the age of nineteen and the other at twenty-two. I always knew that I would not be on welfare forever, and refused to believe that I would be caught up in the welfare trap for another ten years.

In order to break free, I knew that I would have to go to school and acquire job skills. So I did, taking extensive computer training. I put my all into it because I knew that my life and the lives of my children depended on it. I proudly graduated at the top of my class. I landed a job working as a senior administrative assistant making $29,500 a year. That's a big jump from the $3,800 a year that I received while on welfare.

My welfare stint happened about ten years ago. Today,

I am a thirty-eight-year-old proud mother of three beautiful girls who inspire me every day to keep moving in the direction that God is leading me. I know that without God's guidance I would not be here today. I'm also the wife of a wonderful husband who I feel was sent to help me get to the place that God has destined for me. My husband is the support that I so longed for when I was younger.

I was delighted to serve as executive assistant to the president of Bread for the World. Bread has been one of the leading advocates in the fight to improve the welfare system.

I want to thank God (for I know where my help cometh). I also want to thank the taxpayers and Bread for the World members who advocated for funding for the welfare program over the years. I'm going to go on record saying that, one day, I will repay every penny that I borrowed from the government when I was on welfare in the hopes of helping someone else. That is my mission today!

Shortly after Karen wrote this essay, one of her daughters was diagnosed with cancer. Karen had to leave her job to take care of her daughter. Medical expenses and the loss of one parent's income have stalled the upward mobility of Karen's family, but their faith in God and determination to succeed remain intense. Another one of Karen's daughters has enrolled in college.

The world has made—and can make— dramatic progress against hunger.

CHAPTER 3

COUNTRIES THAT
HAVE REDUCED HUNGER
AND POVERTY

The global drive to overcome hunger and poverty in our time is a new phase of the global economic transformation that began with the Industrial Revolution. The Industrial Revolution started in England at the end of the eighteenth century. Innovations in technology and ways of organizing society spawned economic expansion and, over time, social improvements. This revolution spread through the rest of Europe and North America. Eventually, Japan and the Soviet Union mounted huge catch-up efforts.

Since the Second World War the world has been systematically pursuing development, and many developing countries have achieved rapid and sustained economic growth. Countries such as South Korea and Chile have now achieved a much higher level of economic development than countries such as Afghanistan and Bolivia. In some poor countries such as India or Kenya, a large class of people now has a standard of living comparable to the middle class in Europe and the United States.[1] Even among countries that have not achieved much growth, widespread improvements in health and education have taken place.

But even as many poor people have been able to raise their standards of living, economic development has spawned growing inequality in many countries and made the whole world more aware of the extreme gap between rich and poor in the world. Disadvantaged groups and classes of people work—and sometimes fight—to claim a fair share of their nation's wealth and income. Developing nations strive to catch up with the industrialized countries through economic development and by negotiating for more equitable international systems.[2]

This chapter is about seven diverse nations that have made clear progress against poverty—China, Sri Lanka, Ghana, Mozambique, Brazil, Mexico, and the United Kingdom—and about lessons from their experiences.[3]

China

China's progress against poverty has been spectacular. Five hundred million people escaped from extreme poverty between 1981 and 2004. The fraction of China's population in extreme poverty has dropped from two-thirds to one-tenth. China's achievement accounts for most of the global reduction of the number of people in poverty.

China's strides against poverty are partly due to rapid and sustained economic growth. The Chinese economy has expanded by an average of 10 percent per year since the early 1980s.[4] China's embrace of some aspects of capitalism has made it a stronger economic and political power—and, in some ways, a competitor with the United States.

China's increased reliance on markets began in rural areas, where most of China's poor people live. In the 1980s China gradually allowed more families to farm their own plots. Over time the government also allowed rural people to set up their own enterprises or migrate to cities. About half of China's progress against poverty is due to increased reliance on markets in rural areas.[5]

Poor people have also benefited from strong systems of education, health, and social welfare, a legacy from the years when China really was a socialist country. When my wife and I visited China in the early 1980s we were struck that nearly everybody looked healthy and adequately clothed—in contrast to India or Pakistan. Virtually all boys and girls now enroll in school, and 86 percent complete primary school.[6]

China still has big problems, notably its oppressive political system and tremendous environmental problems. Of the world's twenty most polluted cities, sixteen are in China. About 70 percent of the country's lakes and rivers are polluted. Acid rain plagues much of China and reaches into neighboring nations. The United States puts far more strain on the global environment than China, but China is overtaking the United States as the largest producer of greenhouse gases.[7]

When a French journalist named Pierre Haski visited a remote, predominately Muslim village in northern China, an impoverished mother thrust her thirteen-year-old's diaries into his arms, hoping for help. Haski eventually published one of the girl's diaries in the West, *The Diary of Ma Yan*.[8] Yan's diary chronicles her hard life and determination to succeed in school and the hunger that her mother endured to help pay for the girl's schooling.

"I have to study well so that I won't ever again be tortured by hunger or lack of money," writes Yan. China's policies have made it possible for many poor girls to go to school and opened other opportunities for hungry and poor people. But Yan's diary gives us a glimpse into the sacrifice and effort of the many Chinese families who have seized these opportunities and worked their way out of poverty.

Sri Lanka

This island nation just east of India is very different from China, and its pattern of development has also been different. Sri Lanka's poverty rate has been declining for the past two decades, despite a bloody war throughout this period between the government and rebels from the minority Tamil population.

Sri Lanka is a lower-middle-income country, poorer than Mexico or Malaysia, and economic growth has been steady but not rapid. Social programs have been the key to Sri Lanka's social progress. Sri Lanka has long maintained exceptionally strong social programs, including a concerted effort to educate girls. The political will to support these efforts results from a combination of Buddhist culture, a staunch democratic tradition, and social democratic parties. Competition among political parties and an independent press and judiciary have also helped to hold the government and elites accountable to the people.

The civil war was a heavy expense, and the World Bank advised the current government to cut back on social spending. But they maintained or increased spending on social services like education, health, and nutrition. An expanded program of nutrition assistance rapidly reduced deaths among little children and their mothers.[9]

Despite high levels of poverty, the country has one of the

lowest rates of childbirth deaths in the developing world.[10] Literacy and school enrollment rates have improved. Safe water and sanitation systems are widespread. There is more social mobility than in many countries.

The civil war finally ended in May 2009, so Sri Lanka's progress against hunger and poverty should accelerate. On the other hand, the current government is somewhat authoritarian, and human rights abuses have occurred.

Ghana

Ghana is an African success story. In 1992 about 50 percent of the population lived on less than one dollar a day. By 2005 that had dropped to about 30 percent. The country is on track to achieve the first Millennium Development Goal: cutting poverty in half by 2015. After decades of economic decline and dictatorial rule, Ghana has achieved sustained economic growth, effective social programs, and democracy.

Ghana's economy began to expand in the 1980s. Aid donors, impressed by improved development policies, reduced the country's debt and provided substantial assistance.

Ghana returned from military rule to presidential elections in 1992. I lived in Ghana as a young man and returned thirty years later, just before the election of 2000. I was struck by the commitment of grassroots people to democracy. Even people who detested the government in power and thought it was biased against their own ethnic group were ready to accept the election results, one way or the other. The Catholic Church and some Protestant churches were campaigning against corruption to help make democracy work.

Ghana has also developed a strong press and an autonomous election commission. In the election of 2008 a coalition of civil society groups deployed cell phones and personal computers to provide independent information on what was happening at polls across the country. Nine million Ghanaians voted, and the ruling-party candidate lost by just forty thousand votes. Yet he peacefully ceded power to the opposition candidate, John Atta Mills. Northern Ghana has always been much poorer than southern Ghana, and Mills won big in the north.

In the first half of the last decade, Ghana almost doubled the percentage of its national budget devoted to reducing poverty, which included expanded investment in agriculture. In late 2009 the government announced a new strategy to help small-scale farmers become more productive and find markets for their crops. The United States and other aid donors have announced their intention to invest in this initiative.

Mozambique

Mozambique is one of the poorest countries in the world. It suffered a long civil war, financed partly by racist governments in Rhodesia and South Africa. But the government of Joaquim Chissano negotiated a peace agreement in 1992, and the violent opposition became the opposition political party. The government's good economic management contributed to rapid economic and social development. Economic growth has averaged an impressive 8 percent per year since 1993,[11] and the rate of poverty has dropped from 70 percent to 50 percent.[12] President Chissano voluntarily stepped down in 2004, a peaceful transition that contributed to continued peace and development.

I met Chissano in Washington and was impressed by his humble manner and commitment. He spoke quietly of his years as a revolutionary and then as president. He communicated deep hope for Mozambique and Africa as a whole. Mozambique is a large, long country, so communication—let alone democracy—is a challenge. The country was fortunate to have a president of Chissano's moral character.

When I later visited Mozambique I came to know many grassroots people who have contributed in their own ways to Mozambique's progress against poverty. Pedro Kumpila is a prime example.

Pedro's family fled to Tanzania during the war for independence, and Pedro spent most of his first fourteen years there. He returned home, but had to flee violence again—first to wilderness areas and then back to Tanzania. Once peace was established in 1992 Pedro's family came back and rebuilt their lives. Pedro and his wife, Veronica, have four beautiful children, now ages thirteen to twenty.

When the AIDS epidemic came to rural Mozambique, people had no idea what was causing it. Many people suspected their family members of witchcraft. Parents with the disease could not work in their fields, and children were orphaned. Although Pedro's family was not affected, Pedro wanted to help his community deal with this plague, so he took the lead in getting his church to start an AIDS action team.

Team members went door-to-door to talk with families about HIV, how to avoid it, and how to find out if you have it. Now that medication for HIV/AIDS is available, team members help patients travel to the clinic. Pedro and his team sometimes talk with their local chief about village problems or work through their church's diocesan office to raise issues with the district health office.

President Chissano and Pedro Kumpila have contributed in two very different, but both important ways to Mozambique's development.

Brazil

Brazil is an emerging power in the world. Here, hunger is due to extreme inequality. The richest fifth of Brazil's population owns 61 percent of the country's wealth, while the bottom fifth owns just 3 percent.[13] With the largest population in Latin America, Brazil also has the largest number of hungry people.

In the late 1980s, soon after Brazil emerged from a long period of military rule, I helped the World Bank connect with civil society groups—Catholic and other religious institutions, environmental groups, labor unions, farmer associations, and others. I was struck that nearly all civil society groups were preoccupied by hunger, poverty, and inequality. I met with people who were focused primarily on other issues such as the environment or population growth, but they understood that in Brazil progress on these issues depends on progress against hunger and poverty.

After decades of dictatorship, government workers were used to keeping official business secret, and civil society groups were used to working on their own or protesting from the outside. The strong, often radical civil society movement that grew up under the Brazilian dictatorship helped to achieve democracy. This same movement later brought President Luiz Inácio da Silva—known as Lula—to power.

"If at the end of my term every Brazilian person has three meals a day," said Lula in his inaugural address, "I will have fulfilled my life's mission." He probably won't achieve that goal, but he has already reduced hunger in Brazil and is a champion among the world's political leaders for measures to help reduce hunger globally.

Lula worked for years as a union activist, but his policies as president have been supportive of business, and the economy has thrived. Lula also committed Brazil to Fome Zero—Zero Hunger—and expanded safety-net programs. A new Ministry of Social Development and Hunger Eradication manages many programs, including the Bolsa Familia (Family Grant) programs, which are the government's flagship effort against hunger.

The Bolsa Familia includes food stamps and a gas subsidy. One program provides assistance to families with school-age children, but only if their children regularly attend school. Another program provides assistance to families with small children, but only if the mother regularly takes them to a clinic and participates in nutrition classes. The Bolsa Familia programs have reduced poverty and inequality and improved school attendance and child nutrition.[14]

Lula's antihunger campaign also invites citizens and nonprofit groups to get more engaged. Fome Zero calls upon every Brazilian to play a role in eradicating hunger via a "major national solidarity movement" aimed at those in need of food assistance. Through the Mutirão (community-based collective campaign), Brazilians are urged to donate food and money to local charities or to Fome Zero itself. Some citizens and companies contribute to the government's Fund to Fight and Eradicate Poverty.[15] The National Food Security Council engages civil society in the formulation and evaluation of policy.

Mexico

Mexico has successfully reformed what its government does to reduce hunger and poverty. Traditionally Mexico's antipoverty programs were concentrated in urban areas, even though there was more poverty in rural areas. Their main thrust was subsidies for tortillas and other food, which benefited many people who weren't poor. Successive governments launched their own programs to benefit the groups that voted for them, and corruption in the administration of social programs often occurred.

Mexico's renewed effort to fight hunger and poverty began in economic and social crisis. In 1994 violence erupted in Chiapas, a poor southern state where much of Mexico's indigenous population lives. In 1995 the country suffered a financial and economic crisis. The political climate was also changing: Mexico's long-term ruling party, the Partido Revolucionario Institucional (PRI), was losing control while state governments were becoming more important.

In 1996 the government eliminated food subsidies and launched a new program called Oportunidades ("opportunities"). Oportunidades provides subsidies to families, but (like the Bolsa programs in Brazil) only if the families keep their children in school and get them regular medical attention.

The program combined decision making at the top of the federal government with decentralized implementation. Oportunidades initially focused on a small number of rural areas, which allowed it to develop in a disciplined way, relatively free of the corruption that had marred earlier programs. From the beginning the program included a system to evaluate impact.

In 2000 a non-PRI candidate won the presidency for the first time in almost seventy years. President Vicente Fox represented the Partido Acción Nacional (PAN). Oportunidades had demonstrated its effectiveness, and the Fox government continued to expand it. By 2005 it was operating everywhere in the country. One in four Mexicans receive assistance through Oportunidades.

In 2006 Felipe Calderón, now leading the PAN party, narrowly defeated Andres Obrador of the Partido de la Revolución Democrática (PRD). The PRD is strong in the poor southern states of Mexico and promised to expand what the government does for poor people. Obrador disputed the election, and his PRD staged big and disruptive demonstrations in Mexico City. Oportunidades has benefited from ongoing political pressure to reduce poverty, coupled with minimal political interference in how the program operates.[16]

The achievements of Oportunidades are well documented and impressive:

— Families in Oportunidades have more money to spend, and their purchases include more and better food.
— Families are using preventive health services and are healthier.
— Fewer babies are dying, child development has improved, and more children are going on to secondary school.
— Child malnutrition has dropped, and nutritional supplements are providing Vitamin A and folic acid to children.[17]

Mexico's economy has gone through booms and busts, but income per capita has grown by an average of 1.7

percent annually since 1990.[18] The flow of migrants to the United States has helped. In 2007, family members abroad sent $25 billion back to Mexico.[19] On the other hand, the violent gangs that grew up around the sale of drugs into the United States are a fearsome problem.

United Kingdom

The United Kingdom also has been making progress against poverty. Even before its recent efforts, the United Kingdom had reduced poverty below the levels we take for granted in the United States. But poverty is more widespread than in the rest of northern Europe, and it increased in the United Kingdom in the 1980s and 1990s.

When Tony Blair led the Labour Party to power in 1997 he set the goal of ending child poverty in Britain within twenty years. The government increased the payments it makes to families with children and subsidies for child care. The British government increased the minimum wage and required employers to provide more flexibility to workers with children, and it tightened the enforcement of child support from absent parents.

The government also launched a new program of baby bonds, in which the government gives each newborn a bond that he or she can cash at age eighteen for education or to start a business. Family members can add to the value of the child's account, and the baby bonds have successfully encouraged increased saving.

As of 2008, 1.8 million people, including six hundred thousand children, had been lifted out of poverty. The Conservative Party now also embraces the goal of ending child poverty by 2020. Conservative Party leader David Cameron is adamant:

Poverty is not acceptable in our country today. Not when we have people who earn more in a lunchtime than millions will earn in a lifetime, not when we understand so clearly how wealth is created and poverty eradicated. I believe that we can make British poverty history.[20]

Recession has been a big setback, but the coalition government elected in 2010 remains committed to ending child poverty. As they have cut spending, they increased the child tax credit to protect poor children.[21]

Lessons from Success

If countries as different as these—China, Sri Lanka, Ghana, Mozambique, Mexico, Brazil, and Britain—can reduce poverty, it is possible almost anywhere.

These seven country cases show that economic growth and programs focused on reducing poverty are both necessary. Some people dismiss focused efforts to reduce poverty as wasteful giveaway programs, but such programs and policies need not be inefficient or weaken incentives to work. For others, "economic growth" suggests environmental neglect and trickle-down economics, but growth can be environmentally sustainable and benefit all income groups.

These cases also show that healthy societies are more likely to achieve sustained progress against hunger and poverty. Peace and security were preconditions to progress against poverty in nearly all these societies. Sri Lanka is the only country in this group that improved the conditions of poor people in the midst of ethnic violence. Malaysia isn't featured here, but it's an interesting case because a massive affirmative-action program for a disadvantaged ethnic group—the majority Malays—was a prime driver of Malaysia's overall progress against poverty.

Democracy contributed to success in Sri Lanka, Ghana, Mozambique, Brazil, Mexico, and the United Kingdom. By democracy, I mean not only elections but also respect for civil rights, accountable institutions, and an active civil society. China's lack of democracy leaves it more vulnerable to social turmoil in the future. Indonesia might have been included as a success story, but lack of democracy set the stage for financial crisis, social turmoil, and a resurgence of poverty in the late 1990s.[22]

Environmental neglect can also undercut development over the long term. This is another point of vulnerability for China in particular.

Setting specific goals makes a difference. Brazil committed itself to Zero Hunger, and Lula is enlisting civil society in the Zero Hunger campaign, so that the commitment will outlive his government. The United Kingdom has committed itself to ending child poverty within twenty years, and the two largest political parties are committed to the goal, so effort should continue despite the change of government in 2010.

Most of the seven countries achieved progress against poverty only after a period of severe problems. In China the Great Leap Forward and the Cultural Revolution had been economic and political disasters. Ghana had been through decades of economic decline and dictatorship, Mozambique suffered exploitative colonialism and then sixteen years of warfare, and Mexico went through a severe recession and an uprising in its poorest state. Brazil experienced decades of dictatorship.

In each case, citizens knew their country was in trouble. That set the stage for change. Our own country is at a moment like that now—a teachable moment. Maybe the severe problems we face now can become the launching point for changes that will make the United States a better, stronger nation for many years to come.

Perhaps the main lesson for the United States from these countries that have reduced poverty is the importance of government and political commitment. In every one of these countries, the national government established policies that were designed to reduce poverty. Most of the required effort came from poor people themselves, and businesses and other organizations of society played important roles. But in each case the government maintained a framework for society-wide effort. In most cases, a series of governments sustained the national commitment to development and poverty reduction over a period of decades.

These case studies also demonstrate the important role our government has in poverty reduction around the world. The expansion of development assistance by the United States and the other industrialized countries over the past ten years has powerfully helped to reduce poverty in Ghana, Mozambique, and Sri Lanka. U.S. government leadership has also played a big role in developing an increasingly open international economy, and international commerce has been important to economic progress in all seven of these countries.

PART II

WHERE WE WANT TO GO

CHAPTER 4

THIS IS GOD MOVING
IN OUR TIME

The global escape from hunger and poverty is an economic, political, and cultural movement. The great majority of the earth's people are working hard to escape from economic hardship. Their labors are supported, and sometimes undercut, by massive processes of economic development—factories, farms, mines, and telecommunication; lots of creative people figuring out better ways to do things; and constant debates about the rules of the game.

There's a political dimension to the movement against hunger and poverty. Poor people and their allies all over the world are pushing for rules that will work better for them. Their struggles are interconnected with activism on related issues such as environmental protection and the rights of ethnic minorities. In many countries, overcoming hunger and poverty has become an important goal of the national government.

Also part of this great transformation is cultural change, including profound shifts in what people believe and how they live their lives.

This movement in history is immensely complex, beyond our understanding, and wonderful. I think of it as a movement of God in the world.

This chapter looks back at what the Bible says about God moving in history and about justice toward poor and vulnerable people. It discusses what it means to say that God is moving in our time to overcome hunger and poverty. Finally, the chapter argues that work for justice is a way to connect to God—that we are invited to be part of what God is doing in the world.

Previous chapters of this book were about poverty and policies. This chapter is about the Bible and God. We shift from an understanding of poverty to the imperative to overcome it.

God on the Move

Christians, Muslims, Jews, and many people from other religions or no specific religion look to the Bible as a source of spiritual insight. For many of us, the Bible story is the definitive revelation of God.

According to the Bible, God acts in history. Here is a summary of some of the main twists and turns of Bible history. The dates below are not exact, but I find it helpful to remember that some of the major events took place at intervals of roughly five hundred years:

1. God creates the cosmos, the abundant earth, and human beings. Again and again, people act sinfully and suffer for it. Yet the Lord finds a way to help them.

2. In about 2000 BCE, God calls Abraham and Sarah to leave their home in what is now Iraq, travel to a land of

promise, and live there as nomads. Their great-grandson Joseph is sold into slavery in Egypt by his brothers. God rescues Joseph, but his descendants fall back into slavery.

3. In about 1500 BCE, God calls Moses to lead the people of Israel to freedom and gives them his law in the Sinai desert. It's not clear why the Lord "heard the groaning" (Exodus 2:24) of the slaves when he did and not before. The people wandered in the desert for forty years before they entered the promised land of Israel, a land "flowing with milk and honey."

4. In about 1000 BCE, Israel crowns a king: David. The Lord at first objects to centralized power, but later promises to establish David's throne in perpetuity. Under subsequent kings, the nation falls into idolatry and neglect of poor people, and the Lord punishes them with division, conquest, and exile.

5. In about 500 BCE, the Lord brings some of the exiles back to Jerusalem. This is the second great exodus in their history. They have visions of a radically better future, led by the messiah, a great king in David's line.

6. Yet another five hundred years pass, and Jesus Christ appears on the scene—healing the sick, forgiving sinners, and announcing that God's kingdom is at hand. Jesus is crucified, forgiving his enemies from the cross. His disciples later see and believe that God has raised Jesus from the dead.

7. Jesus' resurrection convinces the disciples that he is the Messiah and that his forgiving death is God's offer of forgiveness and new life to everyone. They take that message to the ends of the known world, establishing a global community of people who believe that Jesus lives in them and look for Jesus to establish God's kingdom on earth.

Clearly, the God of the Bible is engaged in human history. The Bible offers doctrines about God, but they grow out of messy, historical experience—a history just as confusing and contradictory as the recent history of China, Mozambique, or the United States. God's plans are often frustrated; God suffers. Yet God repeatedly finds new ways forward toward a better, more blessed future for humanity. God's involvement in the world continues, now and to the end of time.

The personality of the Lord is consistent over the biblical millennia—patient and forgiving, insistent on morality (especially justice toward people in need), and intolerant of phony gods. Yet the Lord of the Bible is full of surprises. When the Jews are exiles in Babylon, the Lord sends a savior to allow them to return to Jerusalem. But who is that savior? Cyrus, the Persian emperor! The Persians conquered Babylon, and the Persians have a more tolerant policy toward conquered peoples. The prophet Isaiah sees the Lord calling Cyrus to be his servant: "I call you . . . though you do not know me" (Isaiah 45:4). God's movement in history is not limited to the efforts of people who believe in God.

The Bible and Justice for Poor People

Every section of the Bible is clear about our obligation to poor people and about the political dimension of justice for poor people.

The primary revelation of God in the Old Testament is the exodus from Egypt. Moses' message was political and radical: "Let the slaves go free!"

The law God gave to the Hebrews through Moses includes many protections for people in need. For example, it was against the law for a farmer to harvest all the grain from his field, as some grain should be left for poor people to glean. It was against the law to make your servants work every day. Immigrant servants must be allowed to rest on the Sabbath.

Moses taught that idolatry and immorality would lead to violence and loss of the land, while faithfulness to the Lord would lead to blessings in this world:

> The LORD your God will make you abundantly prosperous in all your undertakings, in the fruit of your body, in the fruit of your livestock, and in the fruit of your soil. For the LORD will again take delight in prospering you, just as he delighted in prospering your ancestors, when you obey the LORD your God by observing his commandments and decrees that are written in this book of the law, because you turn to the LORD your God with all your heart and with all your soul.
>
> —Deuteronomy 30:9–10

As the Old Testament is usually arranged, the books of Moses (Genesis through Deuteronomy) are followed by historical books (Joshua through Chronicles). The theme of the historical books is that the people turned away from God and God's law. When kings were faithful and led the nation in obedience, the Lord blessed them. But this faithfulness was the exception rather than the rule.

The kingdom of David broke into two nations, Israel and Judah. People in the ruling class pursued their own interests. Coups and countercoups among them set the stage for military defeats. Most of the prophets lived in this period of decline.

The books of the prophets (Isaiah through Malachi) are a third section of the Old Testament. The prophets called on the people to give up idols and obey the law. They went especially to the kings (the government) to demand justice in the land.

In ancient Israel and Judah, shrines and temples were often set up in groves of trees on the tops of hills. The worship of idols was typically festive, with dancing and sometimes intercourse with temple prostitutes. People prayed for abundant harvests and other blessings. In some cases, the services used the same names for God and some of the same religious language that the prophets used, but what most clearly distinguished the worship of the real God from the worship of idols was an insistence on morality, especially concern about poor people.

The prophets repeatedly insisted that the way to national security and prosperity was to worship the real God and establish justice for poor and needy people. Hear these great pronouncements from the prophet Isaiah:

> Ah, you who make iniquitous decrees,
>> who write oppressive statutes,
> to turn aside the needy from justice
>> and to rob the poor of my people of their right,
> that widows may be your spoil,
>> and that you may make the orphans your prey!
> What will you do on the day of punishment,
>> in the calamity that will come from far away?
> To whom will you flee for help,
>> and where will you leave your wealth?
>> —Isaiah 10:1–3

> Is not this the fast that I choose:
>> to loose the bonds of injustice,
>> to undo the thongs of the yoke,
> to let the oppressed go free,
>> and to break every yoke?
> Is it not to share your bread with the hungry,
>> and bring the homeless poor into your house . . .?
> If you offer your food to the hungry
>> and satisfy the needs of the afflicted,

then your light shall rise in the darkness
and your gloom be like the noonday.
The LORD will guide you continually,
and satisfy your needs in parched places,
and make your bones strong;
and you shall be like a watered garden
like a spring of water,
whose waters never fail.

—Isaiah 58:6–7, 10–12

The Old Testament also includes the Psalms and books on the theme of wisdom. The Lord's special concern for poor people and people in trouble also pervades these books. Proverbs stresses how individual obedience to the law often contributes to an abundant life, while the book of Job struggles with the fact that righteous people sometimes suffer. The main conclusion of the book of Job is that human beings do not know why God allows disease and calamity.

The book of Ruth, a jewel of wisdom, is set in the midst of famine. A poor gentile woman, Ruth more than obeys the law of the Lord. She sacrifices to take care of her needy mother-in-law. Boaz, a prosperous farmer, more than obeys the law about leaving grain for poor people to glean. Ruth and Boaz marry, and the Lord blesses them for their faithfulness.

The New Testament begins with the gospels, four different accounts of the life, death, and resurrection of Jesus. In the gospel of Luke, Jesus announces himself as the embodiment of God's messianic promises, including justice for people in need: "The Spirit of the Lord is upon me, because he has anointed me to bring good news to the poor" (Luke 4:18). Jesus' concern for the poor is emphasized in Luke's gospel, which includes the parable of the Good Samaritan and the story of the rich man and Lazarus.

The story of Jesus feeding the hungry crowd is repeated five times in the four gospels, more than any other miracle:

> Then Jesus called his disciples to him and said, "I have compassion for the crowd, because they have been with me now for three days and have nothing to eat; and I do not want to send them away hungry, for they might faint on the way." The disciples said to him, "Where are we to get enough bread in this desert to feed so great a crowd?" Jesus asked them, "How many loaves have you?" They said, "Seven, and a few small fish." Then ordering the crowd to sit down on the ground, he took the seven loaves and the fish; and after giving thanks he broke them and gave them to the disciples, and the disciples gave them to the crowds. And all of them ate and were filled; and they took up the broken pieces left over, seven baskets full. Those who had eaten were four thousand men, besides women and children.
>
> — Matthew 15:32–38

When Jesus envisions the final judgment, he says that our worth will be assessed according to whether we have helped people in need:

> "When the Son of Man comes in his glory, and all the angels with him, then he will sit on the throne of his glory. All the nations will be gathered before him, and he will separate people one from another as a shepherd separates the sheep from the goats, and he will put the sheep at his right hand and the goats at the left. Then the king will say to those at his right hand, 'Come, you that are blessed by my Father, inherit the kingdom prepared for you from the foundation of the world; for I was hungry and you

gave me food, I was thirsty and you gave me something to drink, I was a stranger and you welcomed me, I was naked and you gave me clothing, I was sick and you took care of me, I was in prison and you visited me.' Then the righteous will answer him, 'Lord, when was it that we saw you hungry and gave you food, or thirsty and gave you something to drink? And when was it that we saw you a stranger and welcomed you, or naked and gave you clothing? And when was it that we saw you sick or in prison and visited you?' And the king will answer them, 'Truly I tell you, just as you did it to one of the least of these who are members of my family, you did it to me.'"

—Matthew 25:31–40

The primary revelation of God in the New Testament is the death and resurrection of Jesus. For Christians, Jesus' death and resurrection have cosmic and personal significance. In that event, God broke through sin and death to connect with humanity—and with each of us.

Jesus' death and resurrection also have a political meaning. Marcus Borg's book *Meeting Jesus Again for the First Time* helped me understand Jesus' challenge to laws and political authorities.[1] In Jesus' time, church and state were less separate than in our society. The religious authority (the Sanhedrin) was connected to the national and imperial authorities (King Herod and Pontius Pilate). Jesus disobeyed and taught people to disobey laws that stood in the way of healing or that marginalized people. He healed diseased people on the Sabbath day, teaching that the Sabbath was made for people, not people for the Sabbath (Mark 2:27). He broke purity rules to reach out to lepers, public sinners, and women. The rules that Jesus challenged were not just religious teachings. They were also the law of the land. That is why the Sanhedrin was able to get the Roman authorities to crucify Jesus.

Jesus' resurrection confirms him as God's Messiah and sends his followers into the world. They are given Jesus' Spirit of love for all people and his boldness in the face of authorities.

The book of Acts is about the first years of Christian mission. The early Christians lived under the Roman Empire; they had no influence over laws or involvement in politics. But the apostles' teachings provoked conflict with other religious leaders, and that often got them in trouble with the authorities. Paul, who was a Roman citizen, used his citizenship to advance the cause of the gospel—and ended up being executed by the authorities in Rome.

The gospels and the book of Acts are followed by letters from Paul and other teachers to early churches in the gentile world. The letters urge believers to be models of moral behavior, including active concern for people in need. They also explain that Jesus' forgiving death offers unity with God that does not depend on how moral we are, and that Jesus within us moves us to faithfulness that goes beyond obeying a moral code.

Paul welcomes what governments do to put limits on bad conduct. He writes that governmental authority comes from God (Romans 13). Yet Paul and the other apostolic teachers were clear that a believer's first loyalty is to God and Christ, and that this might lead to trouble with the powers that be and perhaps martyrdom. Some of the New Testament letters were written from jails.

Revelation, the last book of the Bible, is a kaleidoscope of apocalyptic visions. It portrays Rome as decadent and violent, an enemy of God's purposes. Revelation envisions the overthrow of the Roman Empire and the evil it embodies, and the beginning of the reign of Christ. Love and goodness will prevail. In the end, the whole creation will be made new, and even decay will somehow be reversed.

The ambiguous relationship between Christianity and political authority has continued for two thousand years. Since the Roman emperor Constantine converted in 312 CE, Christianity has often been used to help win hearts and minds for a regime in power. On the other hand, Christians and Christian churches have always had a sense of accountability to a higher authority and have often worked to reform the structures and laws of society.

Every book of the Bible—from Genesis to Revelation—is clear that God cares about poor people and social justice. The Bible is not only about social justice, but justice toward people in need is integral to any relationship with the God of the Bible.

God's Presence in the Movement to Overcome Hunger and Poverty

Hundreds of millions of people have escaped from hunger and poverty in our time, and all the nations of the world have acknowledged that further progress is possible. Given what the Bible teaches about God's concern for poor people and God's presence in history, doesn't it make sense to thank God for this great liberation? Doesn't it make sense to see it as an experience of God's saving action in our own history? Isn't God present in whatever efforts we make to help people escape from hunger and poverty?

People who believe in God struggle with suffering. We cannot explain why a good God lets one child die, let alone why tens of thousands of children continue to die needlessly every day. But we believe that God shares in human suffering and brings good out of evil. So we reach out to poor families and pray for their rescue. We pray for progress against poverty with the intensity of a mother who asks God to rescue her own child from a life-saving disease, and people of faith know that God answers prayers in a wonderful way.

Confessing that God is in the movement to end hunger and poverty does not mean that further progress is automatic. The feasibility of ending hunger has been widely recognized for decades. At the World Food Conference of 1973, U.S. Secretary of State Henry Kissinger said that by the year 2000, no child in the world would go to bed hungry. Many reports and conferences since have repeated the claim that we can end hunger, if only we can muster the political will to do it.

I have walked the halls of Congress for hungry people for many years, and there is always something else — some politically important, overriding issue — that politicians feel must take precedence. When the Cold War ended at the beginning of the 1990s, the United States could have redirected more of the massive resources we had spent on the Cold War to overcome hunger and poverty in our country and worldwide. But our nation instead decided not to cut military spending much. In the first decade of this century, a booming economy again gave us additional resources, but we spent them on big tax cuts and the wars in Iraq and Afghanistan.

According to the Bible, God is usually frustrated by the way people and nations behave. People who work for God's purposes in the world must often wait — and sometimes suffer and die for the Lord. As Dr. Martin Luther King Jr. said, "Every step toward the goal of justice requires sacrifice, suffering, and struggle."[2]

Yet God's presence in the movement to overcome hunger and poverty raises our hopes. Some optimism is justified by the experience of recent decades and analysis of what is feasible, and faith in God adds a religious dimension of hope. We believe God has benevolent intentions for humanity and will, in the end, bring us to the day when there will be "hunger no more" (Isaiah 49:10; Revelation 7:16). Through the ups and downs of history, those of us who believe God raised Jesus from the dead are always looking for ways God will bring good out of evil, and we are working to seize those opportunities.[3]

Jim McDonald, my closest colleague at Bread for the World, said it this way in a sermon to his home congregation:

> Even when things seem to be going wrong, when it seems like it's the scoundrels and the scalawags that are in charge, it's good to be reminded that God has other plans, bigger plans, better plans; and God has purposes in mind for this world that even a calamity, whatever its size, whatever its genesis, can't put an end to.[4]

Based on what the Bible says about people in need, doing our part to overcome hunger and poverty is crucial to religious integrity. We can go to church and sing great hymns, but if we don't help people in need, this is made-up religion rather than connection to the real God. We can read spiritual books and pursue a wholesome lifestyle, but if we don't help people in need, our faith remains self-centered.

For people who know and love the Lord, awareness of God's presence in the movement to overcome hunger and poverty adds a dimension of faith that most churchgoers miss. We are connected to God through Jesus Christ, and then see our loving God at work in history. The life of faith becomes exciting and historic, bigger than our private lives. Reading the morning news becomes an extension of our morning prayers. Photos of famine on television are engaging rather than depressing. Our involvement in politics becomes an adventure of faith.

We can share Christian faith in God's love by working for social change in the name of the Lord and making it clear that we see strides against poverty as one aspect of God's gracious presence in the world. Bono, the Irish rock star, says he reconnected with his Christian faith because he was inspired by Christian activists who were working for the cancellation of the debts of poor countries.

Many people who have a hard time making sense of traditional theology understand that the escape of millions of people from extreme poverty is something wonderful, even sacred. Some of the Hebrew people who took part in the original exodus were probably not religiously observant either. But they had an extraordinary experience of the saving God that marked them and their descendants for many generations.

Jesus and His Love

Jesus Christ is my connection point to God. Jesus suffered and died forgiving the people who crucified him. Jesus was God incarnate, so his forgiveness extends to all people. God raised Jesus from the dead, and I experience the Spirit of the living Jesus within me and within the community of Christian believers. I also experience this Spirit in many people who are not Christians and in nature as well.

Many Christians use different language than I do, but all Christianity is grounded in Jesus and his love. Christians experience God's love for them, and we then share God's love with others.

As Paul's letters argue, God in Christ forgives our sins and accepts us as we are—even if we aren't very committed or don't have much faith—and this divine embrace moves us to share the love we receive. The Spirit of Christ within us nudges us to be more generous than we would be on our own.

I experience God's grace as a spring of living water gushing up within me. It is the best thing in my life.

I have not given away all my worldly goods to help people in need. Yet in Jesus Christ I know that God accepts me and uses me anyway. My faith could be stronger, too. But Jesus said that faith the size of a tiny mustard seed can move mountains, and that is my experience.

Some people end up doing very little for people in need because they know they don't have the commitment of a Mother Teresa. Awareness of God's forgiveness allows us to reflect God's goodness in our own halting ways, and God uses even modest acts of faith and compassion to make big changes in the world. God invites us all—gently, patiently—to be part of the great exodus of our time.

It was not obvious that the young Martin Luther King Jr. would be an exceptional religious and political leader. When he decided to go to seminary, ministry was one of the most likely ways an African American man could make a good living. He was serving his first church in Birmingham when Rosa Parks refused to move to the back of a bus. According to historian Taylor Branch, King arrived late to a community meeting that night. When the group decided on a bus boycott, this young Baptist pastor was elected to lead it because the group was sharply divided between two more obvious candidates.

Leading the boycott put huge pressures on King. His telephone rang all day and all night—calls from fellow organizers, calls from cleaning ladies who needed a ride to work so they wouldn't lose their jobs during the bus boycott, and anonymous calls that threatened violence against King and his family.

In the middle of one sleepless night, he had a conversion experience:

King buried his face in his hands at the kitchen table. He admitted to himself that he was afraid, that he had nothing left, that the people would falter if they looked to him for strength. Then he said as much out loud. He spoke the name of no deity, but his doubts spilled out as a prayer, ending, "I've come to the point where I can't face it alone." As he spoke these words, the fears suddenly began to melt away. He became intensely aware of what he called an "inner voice" telling him to do what he thought was right. It was for King the first transcendent religious experience of his life.[5]

Dr. Martin Luther King Jr.'s powerful challenge to our nation emerged from God's presence with him that night.

> **The exodus from hunger and poverty is God moving in our time. Being part of it is important to our spiritual life and to the future of our nation.**

CHAPTER 5

GETTING SERIOUS ABOUT POVERTY WOULD BE GOOD FOR AMERICA

Our country faces big challenges now. We have economic problems, including high unemployment and out-of-control government debt. We don't have as much money as we thought we did a few years ago. Society is deeply divided, our political processes aren't working very well, we are still at war, and our relations with the rest of the world are strained.

A bigger effort to overcome hunger and poverty in our country and worldwide would help our nation cope with these problems and contribute to a more hopeful future for America. This idea comes from the Bible, but you don't have to believe in God to find it convincing.

History Swings on a Moral Hinge

The Bible isn't alone in drawing connections between morality and the prospects of nations. Other ancient texts make the same point. Confucianism, for example, taught that China's empires rose and fell depending on the morality of those in authority. Plato's *Republic* argues that a city ruled by good and wise men will prosper.

Legitimacy is also a theme in modern political science.[1] Some regimes stay in power by sheer force, but people in power almost always seek some moral justification for themselves because legitimacy helps them hold on to power:

> States often resemble banks, which cocoon themselves in pompous buildings and rituals to create an illusion of solidity and to win public confidence, since without that they are remarkably fragile. In the political equivalent of a run on a bank, the astonishing collapse of communist states in Eastern Europe in the early 1990s shows what happens when such legitimacy is lost.[2]

The Hebrew prophets portrayed the Lord moving through history, insisting that nations and kings turn away from idols, immorality, and the neglect of poor people. The prophets speak the word of the Lord about national failings, and that moral word has power. God is patient with evil, and the prophets sometimes wonder out loud, "How long, O Lord?" But in the end, proud empires fall and oppressed people are delivered.

The historical books of the Hebrew scriptures show how the prophets' teaching worked out in practice. When the kings and their nations worshiped carved images or other gods of their own making, they felt less obliged to behave morally, especially toward poor and powerless people. Even members of the royal household pursued their individual interests. As a result, the nations of Israel and Judah suffered from self-serving conflicts among their leaders, with the faction of a prince sometimes inviting a foreign power to come in and help him seize the throne from his father or brother. Over time, such behavior led to political instability, national decline, and domination by foreign powers.

We can see similar patterns in modern history, in the fall of the Soviet Union for example. By the 1970s Communism no longer inspired many people in the Soviet Union. Even people in Moscow's inner circles of power worked the system to their own benefit. Prophetic writers such as Aleksandr Solzhenitsyn did great damage to a tottering system by simply telling the truth. That powerful empire crumbled, mainly from within.

The United States' continued vitality and world leadership depend on our ideals as much as anything else. If people around the world believe that the United States embodies and promotes moral principles, they are more likely to cooperate with us. Even more important, Americans themselves must continue to believe that our country stands for high principles. That conviction makes us and our nation's leaders willing to sacrifice for the larger good. If we think we live in a dog-eat-dog society, we and our leaders are more likely to pursue our individual interests, even at the expense of the nation.

The Old Excuses Are Wearing Thin

The United States is a wonderful country. Its moral strengths include tremendous freedom, creativity, diversity, and democracy. But our country typically gives higher priority to individual liberty, economic growth, and military strength than to helping poor people.

The Luxembourg Income Study, a comparison of poverty in twenty-one relatively high-income countries, sets its poverty line for each country at half of that country's median income. By that measure, the United States has a higher rate of poverty than any other country except Mexico. Not coincidentally, government spending on social programs to reduce poverty is also lower in the United States than in all the other countries except Mexico.[3]

U.S. official development assistance is tiny in relation to our national income—lower than nearly any of the other industrialized countries. If you broaden the analysis to include not just aid, but all the ways that industrialized countries affect developing countries (including trade, security policies, and so forth), the United States still ranks eighteenth among the industrialized countries.[4]

Historically our nation's tendency to neglect poor people has often been justified as a corollary of our love of liberty. For example, Ralph Waldo Emerson argued for "self-reliance" and against charity as a matter of principle:

> Do not tell me, as a good man did today, of my obligation to all poor men in good situations. Are they my poor? I tell thee thou foolish philanthropist that I grudge the dollar, the dime, the cent, I give to such men as do not belong to me and to whom I do not belong.[5]

In *Democracy in America* (1835), Alexis de Tocqueville invented the word "individualism" to describe a cultural trait he noted among Americans. It was rooted in the exceptional drive of people in this young nation toward economic advancement. Tocqueville worried that Americans' excessive preoccupation with their personal affairs could weaken U.S. democracy.

Another well-worn argument against greater efforts to reduce poverty is that free markets will do the job more effectively. Herbert Hoover devoted the final speech of his 1928 presidential campaign to a defense of America's "rugged individualism" as opposed to the "socialism and paternalism" of Europe:

> By adherence to the principles of decentralized self-government, ordered liberty, equal opportunity, and freedom to the individual, our American experiment in human welfare has yielded a degree of well-being unparalleled in the world. It has come nearer to the abolition of poverty, the abolition of fear of want, than humanity has ever reached before.[6]

Hoover's argument won that election, but it didn't ring true any more once the Great Depression hit. Increasing hunger and poverty throughout the early years of the twenty-first century has driven home the point again: free-market policies and economic growth do not automatically open opportunity for everybody.

Neglected Poverty and National Security

In the United States we enjoy extraordinary security. Our country hasn't been invaded by foreign troops for two hundred years, and we can also count on economic and political systems that are stable and work fairly well. In many countries, people suffer huge disruptions in their lives due to massive economic malfunction or disorderly, sometimes violent struggles for power.

But our exceptional security is now somewhat threatened—by serious economic problems, strained relations with the rest of the world, and deep internal divisions. The U.S. public is anxious and is looking to political leaders for solutions.

Our national discussion of these problems focuses on

obvious solutions. To improve the economy, we will need to get macroeconomic management right. To improve international relations, we hope to bring the wars in Afghanistan and Iraq to successful conclusions. To deal with our internal divisions, we look for changed behavior from political leaders and interest groups. But with a cue from the biblical teaching that justice for poor people is important to national security, we can see that an expanded effort to reduce poverty would also help to address each of these big problems that currently threaten U.S. security.

First, the economy will be stronger and more secure for all of us if poor people can participate fully in economic recovery. An economic recovery that leaves much of the U.S. population and many developing countries in financial crisis cannot be robust. When unemployed people get jobs, they contribute to economic production and have income to spend. When dynamic developing economies recover high rates of growth, their increased imports and innovations are tonic for the entire global economy.

Over the long term, improvements in the nutrition, health, and education of poor people generate high returns for everybody. Microsoft founder Bill Gates put it this way:

> Inequity is the most harmful force in the world—not just because it leaves people in misery, but because it wastes human potential and undercuts society's best chance to solve its own problems. As you begin to solve inequity, you decrease the number of problems, and increase the number of problem-solvers. That's why I believe some of the highest-leverage, long-term investments come from improving public education, especially for low-income and minority students, and increasing development assistance for the poorest countries.[7]

President Obama and a Democratic Congress rightly

included investments in poor people in their stimulus program in early 2009, and further antipoverty measures would also be good for the economy as a whole. Bringing deficit spending down is important, too, but that will require attention to the big-ticket elements in the federal budget (taxes, military spending, Social Security, and Medicare). The spending required to boost progress against hunger and poverty is tiny in relation to our $3.5 trillion federal budget.

The link between global poverty and improved U.S. relations with the rest of the world—another big challenge to our national security—is also clear. Poor people throughout the world are struggling for a better life. If the world's superpower is perceived to stand in the way of that better life, we invite resentment and opposition from developing countries. But if the United States deploys its power generously, many people around the world—in the other industrialized countries, too—will cooperate with our country and the international systems in which we have influence.

The United States is especially concerned about its relations with the Muslim world, and more than a third of the people living in absolute poverty in the world are Muslim.[8] Not too long ago I visited two Muslim countries, Turkey and Egypt. Turkey's western cities now remind me of Italy or Spain, and Turkey is eager to join the European Union. Egypt, on the other hand, is poor and threatened by violent strains of Muslim extremism. After visiting these two countries, it is hard to miss the relevance of economic development to U.S. international relations.

Poverty breeds violence. As countries escape from poverty, civil war becomes less likely (see Figure 6).

The problems of poor countries pose other threats to security, too. Susan Rice, U.S. ambassador to the United Nations, explains:

These threats could take various forms: a mutated avian flu virus that jumps from poultry to humans in Cambodia or Burkina Faso; a U.S. expatriate who unwittingly contracts Marburg virus in Angola and returns to Houston on an oil company charter flight; a terrorist cell that attacks a U.S. Navy vessel in Yemen or Somalia; the theft of biological or nuclear materials from poorly secured facilities in the former Soviet Union; narcotics traffickers in Tajikistan and criminal syndicates from Nigeria; or, over the longer term, flooding and other effects of global warming exacerbated by extensive deforestation in the Amazon and Congo River Basins.[9]

Figure 6   **Incidence of Civil War by Country Income,
1960–2006**

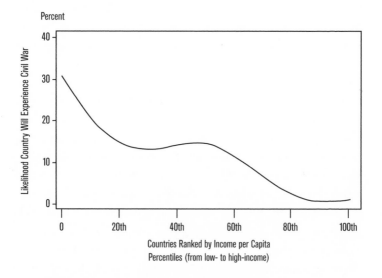

Source: Adapted from Edward Miguel and Chris Blattman, "Civil War," NBER Working Paper #14801, March 2009, 92. Forthcoming, *Journal of Economic Literature.* See http://elsa.berkeley.edu/ ~emiguel/published.shtml, and http://elsa.berkeley.edu/~emiguel/pdfs/miguel_civilwar.pdf.

President Obama's election gave the United States a fresh start in its international relations, and leaders from both parties have supported increases in international development assistance. But little progress has been made toward moderation of the deep and bitter divisions *within* U.S. society and politics—and that may be the most serious threat to U.S. security.

Whether in Washington, DC, or at the local level, liberals and conservatives are still inclined to demonize people on the other side. With Democrats and Republicans unable to work well together, we may be in for several years of political gridlock. A house divided against itself cannot solve its other problems.

Our political divisions grow partly out of class divisions. Over the last twenty-five years the share of income received by the richest 1 percent of the U.S. population has doubled, while median family income has been stagnant, and the real wages of low-income workers have fallen. When Americans are asked if their country is divided between the haves and have-nots, half say yes—up from one-fourth thirty years ago.[10]

Affluent people and their organizations finance candidates, think tanks, lobbyists, and media companies to work for policies that serve their interests. When I visit the Capitol office buildings, the representatives of many special interests are there in force. Special interests make it hard for Congress to tackle many problems, and the influence of money in politics skews the system against changes that would help people who don't have much money. The Supreme Court decision in the case of *Citizens United v. Federal Election Commission* to let corporations contribute directly to political campaigns will make this problem worse.

Understandably, many middle- and low-income people are frustrated with government. They know that government doesn't work very well for them. Some are liberal, and some are conservative; many have become cynical. The great majority of voters have come to agree on one thing: we need change. That's why both candidates in the last presidential election — Barack Obama and John McCain — campaigned as candidates for change.

The only path forward may be for Congress to achieve some real change for the better. If the 2010 reform of health care really improves health care for middle- and low-income people, for example, that will encourage people to work together on other national problems. A more active, positive-minded citizenry will make it tougher for special interests to stand in the way.

If we can achieve changes that reduce hunger and poverty, that would be especially inspiring. We could dramatically reduce hunger among American children, for example. This could be a bipartisan initiative, and it would engage states and community groups in collaboration with federal programs. After three or four years, churches could be telling their members that it's no longer so urgent that they bring groceries to church — that concerned people can turn their attention to tutoring programs and other ways of helping. When that day comes, a lot of Americans — rich, poor, and in between — will feel good about our country and ready to work together on other problems.

If we can get the United States to make a more serious effort to reduce hunger and poverty, our economy will be more dynamic, our relations with the rest of the world improved, and our society more united. Our country will be better — and more secure.

CHAPTER 6

PEOPLE OF FAITH
CAN MAKE
CONGRESS WORK

When asked if I am pessimistic or optimistic about the future, my answer is always the same: If you look at the science about what is happening on earth and aren't pessimistic, you don't understand data. But if you meet the people who are working to restore this earth and the lives of the poor, and you aren't optimistic, you haven't got a pulse. What I see everywhere in the world are ordinary people willing to confront despair, power, and incalculable odds to restore some semblance of grace, justice, and beauty to this world.

Paul Hawken[1]

The experience of Bread for the World over almost four decades demonstrates that people of faith can win political change for hungry and poor people. In Bread for the World's early years, its members were sometimes the only organized grassroots voice speaking up for hungry people, but they won changes that significantly reduced hunger and poverty in the United States and worldwide. Over the last two decades—the part of this history I have lived—the scale of Bread for the World's impact has grown. This experience makes me hopeful that people of faith and conscience can convince our nation now to make a bigger effort to overcome hunger and poverty.

Two Big Victories for Little Children

Arthur Simon, the founder of Bread for the World, was the pastor of a small church in a poor neighborhood of Manhattan. In *The Rising of Bread for the World* (Paulist Press, 2009), Art recalls that he was always responding to the many troubles of poor individuals in his congregation and neighborhood. His congregation also contributed to world hunger appeals. But Art and his brother Paul Simon (later a U.S. senator) were also thinking together about the politics of world hunger, and Art had the idea of a Christian citizens' movement against hunger.

Bread for the World quickly attracted a grassroots network of concerned people from diverse church bodies. They gathered in homes and churches to pray, study the issues, write letters to Congress, and reach out to their congregations and communities. The organization didn't have much money and didn't do much marketing. Each year, Bread asked congregations across the country to take up an offering—not of money, but of letters to Congress.

Bread's network of activists and churches built a track record of legislative successes. Their biggest achievements in the 1970s and 1980s were the Women, Infants, and Children Supplemental Nutrition Program (WIC) and programs to reduce child deaths in developing countries.

Bread members campaigned throughout those early years to build strong bipartisan support and funding for WIC. The program now reaches 9 million mothers, infants, and children in this country who would otherwise lack adequate nutrition. WIC for pregnant women reduces the proportion of low-birth-weight babies by 25 percent. The General Accounting Office estimates that every dollar spent on WIC for pregnant women saves taxpayers at least $2.84 in Medicaid costs in the first two months after childbirth. WIC also demonstrably reduces nutrition-related illnesses among the little children in the program.[2]

During the recession of the early 1980s, the United Nations Children's Emergency Fund (UNICEF) proposed a strategy to reduce child deaths in developing countries. Jim Grant, then head of UNICEF, talked about the possibility of a "child survival revolution." Technological advances in vaccines had made it easier to inoculate children. UNICEF also proposed to teach poor parents simple strategies that could keep many children from dying. For example, a solution of sugar and salt in water can stop diarrhea from killing a child.

Bread for the World's members across the country urged Congress to back the Child Survival Revolution, and Congress provided a growing stream of funding. Over the years, child survival programs have dramatically reduced child deaths. Half as many children die from diarrhea now. More than 100 million children in developing countries are immunized every year, and child inoculation campaigns helped eradicate smallpox from the face of the earth.[3]

From the outset, Bread for the World was a model of civility and worked in a bipartisan way. Bread and its members reached out to churches, and most congregations, thankfully, include Republicans and Democrats. Also, members of Congress from the two parties have often worked together for hungry people. When that happens they merge liberal and conservative concerns in ways that make policies effective and win broad political support.

I became president of Bread for the World in 1991. During the 1990s, one of Bread's campaigns helped shift U.S. policy in the Horn of Africa. During the Cold War, the United Nations had supported dictators in the region, vying with the Soviet Union for bases on the Red Sea. The Bread for the World legislation mandated U.S. support for peace, development, and democracy and allowed a quick start to U.S. aid after a change of government in Ethiopia.

Another Bread campaign stopped the decline in U.S. funding for agricultural development in Africa. We increased funding for WIC, Head Start, and Job Corps. We were not able to increase international development assistance in the 1990s, but we did help achieve needed reforms at the World Bank.

We tried and failed to stop the welfare reform bill of 1996. Welfare reform did some good, but that one bill also slashed $60 billion over five years from programs to help poor people. Fortunately, we managed to maintain the rules that make SNAP responsive to need. If need increases, the program expands automatically without requiring further action from Congress. That has made SNAP a lifeline for millions of families during this recent time of high unemployment. When the massive oil spill of 2010 depressed the economy in U.S. communities along the Gulf of Mexico, SNAP expanded quickly to help families in need.

Jubilee

The Jubilee campaign to cancel the debts of some of the world's poorest countries was a turning point in the politics of world hunger. Many of the world's poorest countries were saddled with unpayable debts. Some of them sent more money to rich countries to pay back old debts than they spent on the health and education of their people.

In 1998 Pope John Paul II and Archbishop Desmond Tutu both suggested that the millennium year, 2000, be celebrated by canceling the debts of poor countries. They referred to the book of Leviticus in the Bible, which called for a jubilee every fifty years. In that jubilee year, all debts would be forgiven and the land returned to its original owners. The idea had power, and British activists began to organize the international Jubilee campaign.

In the United States, Jim McDonald from Bread for the World chaired the legislative coalition, working closely with staff from church bodies. Catholics, Lutherans, Episcopalians, and Presbyterians—and Oxfam America, an international development charity—were core partners.

The U.S. groups adapted to U.S. political realities. In other international campaigns—the campaign to ban land mines, for example—U.S. groups followed their European colleagues too closely. In the end, nearly all the nations of the world signed a treaty to ban land mines, but the United States did not sign, which undercut the treaty's effectiveness.

In the Jubilee campaign, Bread for the World and the church bodies who worked with us did not agree with our international partners to push for unconditional debt cancellation for all low-income countries. We wanted a mechanism that would achieve a jubilee for poor people in low-income countries, not just debt reduction for their governments. We also knew we couldn't possibly convince the U.S. Congress to approve unconditional debt cancellation. Discussions in my office contributed to the eventual solution—debt reduction for countries with credible poverty reduction strategies.

The Clinton administration wasn't initially interested, and we had no supporters in Congress. But church people in Birmingham, Alabama, recruited an unlikely champion: Representative Spencer Bachus.

Pat Pelham was a young mother in Birmingham. She was moved during her morning prayers to do something for people in Africa. Her husband's job and two small children put going to Africa out of the question. A minister at her church, Independent Presbyterian, suggested she get their church involved in Bread for the World. Pat and her friend Elaine Van Cleave came to a meeting with me at Our Lady of Sorrows Catholic Church. Father Martin Muller had invited me to speak.

Pat and Elaine organized a hunger committee at Independent Presbyterian. They invited their member of Congress, Spencer Bachus, to an evening event. I sat on his left, and a church member who chairs the local Republican Party sat on his right.

Several years later, at the beginning of 1999, Bachus was appointed chair of the international subcommittee of the House Financial Services Committee. If Congress was going to approve debt relief for poor countries, it would have to start in Bachus's subcommittee.

I called Pat right away. Our Lady of Sorrows asked people to sign a petition the next Sunday. Pat, Elaine, and two friends from their church flew to Washington at their own expense to bring the petition and talk with Representative Bachus.

Elaine explained why they had come. "I don't know much about economics or international finance," she began. "But I do know that tens of thousands of children die every day from hunger and other preventable causes. As a mother, that really bothers me. Most of the time, I think there is nothing we can do about it. But it would help a lot if you would sponsor this Jubilee legislation."

Bachus became Congress's most effective advocate for debt relief for the world's poorest countries.

The Jubilee campaign was strong in Europe, so the Clinton administration was also under pressure from other governments in the G8, the club of the world's eight most powerful economies. But Treasury Secretary Lawrence Summers told me twice that the support of Spencer Bachus, a conservative Republican, convinced him to urge President Clinton to support poor-country debt cancellation.

Bachus is a Southern Baptist. He believes in heaven and hell. At one hearing on poor-country debt, Bachus said, "If we don't write off some of this debt, poor people in these countries will be suffering for the rest of their lives — and we'll be suffering a lot longer than that."

He held up a statement from Pope John Paul II and said, "I haven't read much by Catholics before, but I don't know how any Christian could read what the pope is saying here and not agree that we need to do something about the debt of these countries."

Representative Jim Leach, a moderate Republican from Iowa, also provided crucial leadership. He chaired the entire Financial Services Committee. Bread for the World staff couldn't get in to see him. His staff insisted that the chairman was preoccupied with more important legislation.

But Tom Booker and other Bread for the World members got an appointment with Leach back home in Iowa City. Their appointment was late in the day, and Leach was running late. So Leach invited Tom to ride with him to the airport. Tom was not at all sure of himself, but he explained the idea of Jubilee.

When staff from Bread for the World and two church bodies finally got in to see Leach in Washington a month later, Leach immediately offered to sponsor the legislation. Leach's staffer was sitting next to me and literally almost fell off his chair in surprise.

The Financial Services Committee passed the debt-relief bill two weeks before the G8 Summit in the summer of 1999. The proposal that President Clinton brought to the Summit became the international debt relief initiative. By September the U.S. Treasury had won international agreement on reforms at the World Bank and International Monetary Fund. The Bank and IMF were instructed to focus the benefits of debt relief on the reduction of poverty and to encourage democratic processes to help develop poverty reduction strategies in these countries.

Congress as a whole still had to approve and fund U.S. participation in international debt relief. Bachus lobbied his conservative colleagues, and Pat and Elaine kept up their grassroots work back in Birmingham. They engaged other churches in writing letters to Bachus, organized an event at the local Baptist university to honor him, and convinced the *Birmingham News* to praise his leadership on this issue.

"I really hadn't thought much about places like Africa before," Bachus says frankly. But he had come to see the world differently because of church people back home.

In November 1999, Bono—lead singer of U2—made his first lobbying visit to Washington. Bono's advisors on Africa issues, Jamie Drummond and Bobby Shriver, convinced him that the international Jubilee campaign couldn't succeed without support from the U.S. Congress.

Bobby Shriver had a relationship with Representative John Kasich, chair of the House Budget Committee. Kasich hosted Bono's first visit to Congress and arranged for him to meet other key Republicans, including Senator Jesse Helms, the arch-conservative chair of the Foreign Relations Committee. Bread for the World organized a press event for Bono and U.S. church leaders outside St. Peter's Catholic Church, just south of the Capitol.

Big policy changes typically require many steps, and we needed to keep pushing throughout the year 2000. The campaign gained broad support. But Senator Phil Gramm, chair of the Senate Banking Committee, was still dead set against the idea, and there was no way around him.

In November 2000, Representative John Kasich helped organize an unusual meeting in the Cabinet Room of the White House. President Clinton led the meeting. Key Republicans and Democrats from Congress were there. Five religious leaders were also around the table. We talked about how to win final passage for debt-relief funding. I closed the meeting with a prayer.

I then scooted around the table to talk with President Clinton. I caught up with him as he was speaking to Rev. Pat Robertson, a leader among politically active Christian conservatives. Robertson hadn't been involved in Jubilee, but that meeting convinced him to speak in favor of debt relief for poor countries on his *700 Club* television program. He told his viewers in Texas to contact Senator Gramm, and that was the unexpected help we needed. The debt-relief bill passed.

The White House invited me to introduce President Clinton at the signing ceremony. The president looked at Spencer Bachus and said, "Without your leadership, we wouldn't be here today." I used my two minutes to talk about the essential involvement of grassroots people and churches across the country. I specifically mentioned Pat Pelham, Elaine Van Cleave, and Father Martin Muller.

The Jubilee Campaign of 1999–2000 started a process that has reduced the debt obligations of thirty relatively well-governed poor countries by $78 billion. They are paying $3 billion less in debt service every year, and the increase in their annual funding for basic health and education has been more than that.[4] Debt relief was the initial source of funding for the dramatic expansion of school enrollment in Africa.

Because we stressed grassroots participation in our

Jubilee bill, the World Bank now encourages all poor-country governments to involve civil society in developing poverty reduction strategies. Religious bodies, farmer organizations, and groups that focus on environmental or gender issues are invited to share their perspectives with government officials. Although these consultation processes vary in effectiveness, they have improved planning, strengthened democracy, and reduced corruption in some countries.

Tens of thousands of Christians across the United States urged their members of Congress to support the Jubilee legislation of 1999 and 2000. Several thousand people were just as active as Pat Pelham and Elaine Van Cleave. In all, we think Congress received about 250,000 letters in support of Jubilee. Bono made several trips back to Washington, national church leaders spoke out, and political leaders from both parties helped get the job done. Jubilee campaigners were also active in Europe and some of the countries that received debt relief.

Yet I am struck by the pivotal role Pat and Elaine played. It is hard to imagine how the debts of poor countries would have been reduced if Pat hadn't been moved by her prayers to push for an unlikely change in U.S. politics. Millions of smiling African girls are proudly wearing school uniforms and learning to read today, partly because Pat Pelham and Elaine Van Cleave dared to believe we could get Congress to do the right thing.

Nutrition Assistance and Development Assistance

During the first decade of this century—a time when U.S. politics was less focused on the needs of poor people than now—Bread for the World helped to more than double funding for the national nutrition programs and triple funding for effective programs of international development assistance.

In the wake of huge cuts to the food stamp program as part of welfare reform, the national organizations that focus on domestic hunger worked to repair some of the damage. These groups include food banks, church groups, and other advocacy organizations. The national nutrition programs expanded, partly because of improvements we won in Congress and partly in response to growing poverty.

Between 2000 and 2009 federal spending on food for poor people increased from $33 billion to $80 billion. The SNAP program alone expanded to reach 16 million more people. The nutrition programs moderated the increase in hunger over the course of the decade and helped millions of families cope when recession hit.

Bread for the World members also campaigned over the decade to increase funding for those foreign aid programs that are focused on promoting development and reducing poverty. We received surprising help from both President Bush and Bono—stories I'll tell in the next chapter. But grassroots advocates also played an essential role. As Bono says, "Politicians are glad to appear with a celebrity, but they get scared when they also hear from preachers, soccer moms, and college students across the country."

Congress tripled appropriations for poverty-focused development assistance over the decade—from $7.5 billion in 2000 to $22.0 billion in 2010. These figures come from Bread for the World's own, well-established system of tracking funding for those foreign aid programs which, in our judgment, focus mainly on development and poverty reduction. The African countries that have achieved rapid economic growth and better government were supported by increasing aid from the United States and the other industrialized countries.

One of the grassroots heroes for increased development assistance was Connie Wick. I first heard her name in the White House.

President Bush was signing an Africa trade bill that Bread for the World had helped through Congress. I seized the chance to speak with him about funding for the Millennium Challenge Account, a new channel for aid to poor countries that he had proposed.

"Thank you for helping to pass this Africa bill," I said. "We also need your help in getting Congress to approve the full amount you've requested for the Millennium Challenge Account."

"How much are we short? A billion?" asked President Bush.

"A billion and a half," I replied.

The president didn't move away, so I continued, "You need to get a senator who will treat the Millennium Challenge Account like his own baby. Nobody in the Senate is really fighting for the funding."

President Bush pointed across the room at Senator Richard Lugar. Lugar is a senior Republican member of the Senate and was then chair of the Foreign Relations Committee. Bread for the World has rallied around Lugar's leadership on many issues of importance to hungry people in this country and worldwide. The president walked over to talk with Lugar, pulling me along.

Senator Bill Frist, then majority leader, heard the president's voice and joined us. The president put one hand on my shoulder and the other on Senator Lugar's shoulder. He urged that the Senate provide the funding he had requested for the Millennium Challenge Account. When the president and Senator Frist stepped away, Senator Lugar stayed to talk a bit longer.

"I was just answering a letter from a constituent, Connie Wick," said Lugar, "and she was saying—well, she was also urging us to fully fund the Millennium Challenge Account."

When I got back to our office, I learned that Connie Wick was a Bread for the World member in her mid-eighties. She had for many years led the Bread group at the Robin Run Retirement Center in Indianapolis. She has since died, but the Robin Run group still meets monthly to write letters to Congress. They also invite candidates for public office to speak at the center.

Lugar knew and respected Connie Wick. I had watched the president of the United States working to influence the Senate majority leader and the chair of the Senate Foreign Relations Committee. And what was in Senator Lugar's mind just then? He was trying to remember what Connie Wick thought about this issue.

The Farm Bill and Economic Turmoil

Emboldened by success, Bread for the World has been taking on bigger, tougher issues. One of them is the Farm Bill, which is rewritten about every five years. Bread for the World decided, with some trepidation, to campaign for broad reform of the Farm Bill in 2007. The Farm Bill sets policies for important nutrition programs, and farm policies themselves are also important to hungry and poor people. Most of the farm subsidies go to affluent landowners, so the money could be redirected to do more for farm and rural people who really need help. Also, farm payments and protectionism in the industrialized countries have long frustrated agricultural development among poor rural people in Africa and other parts of the developing world.

At the Senate Agriculture Committee's first hearing on the Farm Bill, I testified alongside the presidents of the nation's three main farm organizations: the Farm Bureau, the National Farmers Union, and the National Farmers Organization. The farm groups were all pushing for increases in the big subsidies that go to five commodities: corn, wheat, soybeans, rice, and cotton. Chairman Tom Harkin graciously thanked me for "speaking truth to power." Bread for the World and our church allies forged a coalition with environmental groups (because the commodity subsidies contribute to environmental damage) and taxpayer groups (because the subsidies are a waste of taxpayer dollars). Together, we mounted a serious challenge to the abusive features of the current system of farm subsidies.

When other church leaders and I went to see Senate Majority Leader Harry Reid, he was candid. "The commodity groups are one of the most powerful lobbies in Washington. They go to every fund-raiser. They have friends on both sides of the aisle." The commodity groups spent $80 million in Washington in 2007 to defend the subsidies.[5]

The Corn Growers Association managed to win a major increase in subsidies and trade protection for corn ethanol in a separate piece of legislation. For decades, farm subsidies had depressed grain prices worldwide. Now the ethanol subsidies combined with other factors to provoke a sudden increase in the prices of basic grains and in world hunger.

House Speaker Nancy Pelosi was convinced that reducing farm subsidies would cost the Democrats needed rural seats in the 2008 election. Bread and its partners wanted to shift money within the Farm Bill from the commodity subsidies to better purposes. But she protected the subsidies and found money outside the Farm Bill for the other things we wanted to do—in effect, buying off most of the Democrats who might have voted for reform. Representative Jim

McGovern, a great advocate for hungry people, negotiated a big increase for nutrition assistance. The final Farm Bill also increased funding for minority farmers, rural development, and conservation.

These improvements in the Farm Bill would not have been achieved without our campaign. But we failed to get Congress to shift to a fairer system of support for farmers.

As the Farm Bill was being finalized, grain prices were soaring and world hunger was sharply increasing. In the White House, the State Department, and wherever I could get a hearing, I called attention to this crisis. I was interviewed twice by Bill Moyers on public television, Bread for the World mounted a Web campaign, and many members contacted Congress once a week for several months to raise the alarm about the price-driven surge in world hunger.

Congress wasn't interested in reversing the decision it had just made to promote the diversion of corn into ethanol or in modifying the Farm Bill to promote food production globally. But President Bush and Congress agreed on an emergency appropriation of $1.9 billion in food and agricultural assistance to countries where hunger had suddenly increased.

The organizations that protect subsidies to affluent farmers have proved too strong for us, at least for now. But looking back over Bread for the World's nearly four decades of history, the main lesson is that grassroots people—people like you and me—can often sway Congress to make changes that help millions of hungry people.

> **People of faith and conscience can have an impact on the politics of hunger.**

JOE MARTINGALE,
A BALANCED LIFE

Joe Martingale grew up in Brooklyn, New York, one of nine children in a Catholic working-class family. His father was a longshoreman, and although they weren't exactly poor, they "didn't have anything extra."

Joe benefited from a good education. He attended Catholic schools and, after four years in the navy, graduated from St. Francis College in Brooklyn Heights. Joe earned his law degree at Columbia University.

He went on to have a successful career. He was a lawyer on Wall Street, then an executive for JC Penney, and ended up spending most of his working life as a healthcare consultant.

He was surrounded by ambitious New Yorkers. To most of the people he worked with, "Billable time was everything," says Joe. "The pressure to have a lot of billable time and develop new business pushes people over the edge in how they run their lives."

But Joe always knew there was more to life than the bottom line. He remembered the working-class people from his boyhood neighborhood, those who were sometimes barely keeping food on the table. He also remembered the lessons he learned about "what was important" from his mother and his Catholic education—namely, caring for others, especially hungry and poor people.

Joe and his wife, Mary, have consistently given away a large percentage of their income. Some years they have donated as much as 50 percent of their income, and never less than 25 percent, to Bread for the World and other organizations that help hungry and poor people. Joe insists that because he was lucky enough to earn a good salary, "the sacrifice was never great."

Joe also dedicated as much of his time to serving hungry

and poor people as he did to his high-paying, high-pressure career. Mary and Joe volunteered at an overnight shelter for homeless women run by a local Methodist church. He was inspired by how his fellow volunteers, who he describes as "salt-of-the-earth working people, veterans, marines," kept the ministry running, although many of them were struggling to make ends meet themselves.

For more than twenty years, Joe and Mary spent several nights a month staffing the twelve-bed facility. He would serve a meal and sleep at the shelter, then rush home to shower and change, and hurry off to catch a plane for a business trip or get to a downtown meeting.

One night at the shelter, he watched an old woman struggle down the steep stairs to the church basement. She had been living on the streets for many years and, like the others at the shelter, came looking for a hot meal and a safe place to sleep for the night.

"She was eighty-nine years old," Joe recounted with emotion in his voice. "I looked at her, and she reminded me of my own mother, who was of the same generation. I thought, 'What is wrong with our country?' I just couldn't imagine that with all our wealth, this eighty-nine-year-old woman could be left to scramble for a bed at night."

For Joe, the question "What is wrong with our country?" wasn't just rhetorical. Since the early 1980s he had been part of Bread for the World, urging his members of Congress to address the needs of hungry and poor people in the United States and around the world.

He first heard of Bread from an article in the Catholic magazine published by the Maryknoll Fathers. Intrigued by the idea of getting at the root causes of hunger and poverty, Joe began his support with a regular check. Before long, he and Mary also joined a Bread for the World group in New York. By the time Joe attended his first Bread for the World Lobby Day and visited the offices of his members of Congress in Washington, DC, he was hooked.

Although his senators agreed in principle that caring for hungry and poor people was important, they often needed a little reminding to sign on to a particular piece of legislation that would help hungry people. Joe's representative was a different story—he rarely supported bills that Bread for the World supported. Yet Joe visited his office faithfully year after year—often alone—urging support of measures that would help hungry families. Some years he was able to bring hundreds of letters of support from other constituents in the district, but Joe was never able to influence his representative's position. In all the years that Joe visited this representative's office, he was always seen by an aide and never got to meet with the man personally.

Now Joe has a new representative in the House who is usually more receptive. But he doesn't see those frustrating hours he spent every year communicating with his previous representative's office as wasted. Joe's involvement in legislative advocacy isn't just about winning. It is about being faithful.

Joe doesn't wear his Christianity on his sleeve. But it has clearly shaped his values and how he lives. For Joe, advocating for hungry people carries great value: "Bread for the World allows you to become spiritual in a subtle way. It doesn't always need to be expressed in an outward prayer. But it is a very satisfying experience to know what you are working on is a manifestation of the gospel. For me, involvement in Bread is almost selfish. I want to be on the 'right side.' And if you read the Bible, many of the lessons have to do with poor and hungry people."

Joe has had a big impact among hungry and poor people—the thousands he reached through his many nights at the homeless shelter, and the millions he has touched by helping to pass antihunger legislation. Joe has also had an influence on others through hundreds of talks at churches in New York. Now nearing retirement, Joe realizes that he has also had an influence on many young associates he mentored in his professional life—always reminding them that while work and success are important, even more important is to find balance and a deeper meaning.

How to Influence Your Member of Congress

If you are writing to your member of Congress, keep it short and be sure to include your name and address (to show that you are a constituent). State succinctly what action you want your member of Congress to take and why this is important to you.

Handwritten letters are effective. President Obama asks his staff to bring him ten handwritten letters every day—not copies of e-mails—as a way of staying in touch with people.

Mail to Congress takes about a week longer than other mail, because it is radiated as a security measure. So if your message is urgent, call your member's Washington office or send an e-mail.

If you send an e-mail, don't just forward an e-mail you receive from somebody else. Use a different subject line, include your return address, and make it personal. Congressional offices are struggling to cope with the rising flood of e-mail, and offices don't give much attention to mass e-mails and postcards.

You'll have an even bigger impact if you organize letter writing in your church or group. You'll also have a big impact if you seek a meeting with your member of Congress or an advisor.

Pray for your members of Congress.

CHAPTER 7

HOPEFUL DEVELOPMENTS
IN U.S. POLITICS

*Keep fightin' for freedom and justice, beloveds, but don't you forget to
have fun doin' it. Lord, let your laughter ring forth. Be outrageous,
ridicule the fraidy-cats, rejoice in all the oddities that freedom can
produce. And when you get through kickin' ass and celebratin' the
sheer joy of a good fight, be sure to tell those who come after how much
fun it was.*

—Molly Ivins[1]

W HEN I came to Bread for the World in 1991, few
groups organized advocacy for hungry and poor
people. My main innovation was to set aside some of Bread
for the World's resources to encourage and help other
organizations to get involved in the politics of hunger and
poverty. Our goal has been to build a movement strong
enough to push the U.S. government to do its part to overcome mass hunger and poverty.

While we were expanding the movement, powerful
help was on the way from unlikely quarters. As the new

century began, we found ourselves working with Bono and other celebrities on global poverty issues. We started getting help from some wealthy people, notably Bill and Melinda Gates. Evangelical Protestants and Jewish and Muslim organizations became more engaged in advocacy for poor people. And each of the country's last three presidents have, in different ways, provided leadership on these issues.

These changes add up to a positive shift in U.S. politics around hunger and poverty issues. U.S. politics has also become more polarized, and Americans feel frustrated with our government and politicians. But we have some momentum as we push for an expanded national effort to reduce hunger and poverty in poor countries and the United States.

Building the Movement to Overcome Hunger and Poverty

Twenty years ago, few of the U.S. charities that help hungry and poor people in this country and around the world were involved in advocacy. Charities helped poor people, but thought they couldn't and shouldn't get involved in politics. That has changed, and Bread for the World encouraged the change. We argued that charities should speak up for the people they serve. We wrote about this and convened meetings about it.

As key charities started to expand their involvement in advocacy, Bread for the World helped them. I have served for many years as a board member of InterAction, the association of U.S. charities that work in developing countries, and Bread for the World staff helped plan their first events on Capitol Hill. InterAction and some of its member charities are now major partners in advocacy. We also partnered with Feeding America, the main network of U.S. food banks and food charities, as they expanded their involvement in advocacy. We worked with them on Washington events and legislative campaigns.

Bread for the World has also had some influence on Catholic Charities, World Vision, Lutheran World Relief, and MAZON (the main Jewish antihunger organization)—urging them to put more effort into advocacy and collaborating as they did so. The rapid development of Web-based advocacy made it easier for organizations to mobilize letters to Congress from their supporters.

Bread for the World has engaged in ongoing analysis of what it would take to end widespread hunger and poverty in the United States and around the world—in effect, planning the movement we hoped would emerge. Based on that analysis, we called together diverse institutions that might become interested in forming an Alliance to End Hunger. They included diverse religious groups, charities, foundations, corporations, unions, universities, think tanks, and advocacy organizations.

I am now president of three affiliated institutions— Bread for the World, which lobbies Congress for hungry people; Bread for the World Institute, a tax-deductible affiliate that does research and education to help end hunger; and the Alliance to End Hunger, our secular affiliate.

The Alliance now has eighty members, including Jewish and Muslim groups, Universities Fighting World Hunger, and concerned corporations such as H-E-B, Sodexo, Cargill, Mosaic, Elanco, and Land O'Lakes. The Alliance is managed by Ambassador Tony Hall, who crusaded for hungry people as a member of Congress for twenty-four years and then served as U.S. ambassador to the U.N. Food and Agriculture Organization (FAO) and the U.N.

World Food Program. Tony works personally with members of Congress, meeting with them one-by-one to encourage them to step forward as heroes for hungry people. The Alliance helps its members follow hunger issues in Congress and work together.

The Alliance has done a series of studies on how U.S. voters think about hunger and poverty, and we have learned that government initiatives to help hungry and poor people enjoy broad support among both Republicans and Democrats.[2] Yet nearly all Americans believe government initiatives are often ineffective and that the best programs support hard work and self-reliance. Politicians can connect with U.S. voters by putting "liberal" and "conservative" themes together—making clear their commitment to overcoming hunger and poverty but, at the same time, insisting that programs be effective and avoid creating dependency.

The Alliance to End Hunger has shared these findings with politicians across the political spectrum, and several candidates for president in the 2004 and 2008 elections used our findings.

The three U.N. agencies focused on hunger and agriculture—FAO, the World Food Program, and the International Fund for Agricultural Development—joined together to organize an International Alliance Against Hunger. They used our Alliance as one model and encouraged the formation of national alliances against hunger to build political will in other countries around the world. The U.N. Food and Agriculture Organization invited me to give the inaugural lecture at its 2004 biannual meeting. Other lecturers in this series have included John D. Rockefeller, Indira Gandhi, and Julius Nyerere. I was able to talk with representatives of all the nations of the world about building the political will to overcome hunger.

Bono

Bono had his own ideas about how to build political will to help poor people. He played an important role in the Jubilee campaign, and by 2002 he was working with Bread to increase development assistance to Africa. He continues to serve as a powerful voice for Africa, bringing with him a dazzling capacity to command media attention and influence powerful people.

Bono (born Paul Hewson) is the son of a Protestant mother and a Catholic father. He is still married to his high school sweetheart, and he has been part of the same band—U2—for more than thirty years.

During the Ethiopia famine of the mid-1980s, another Irish rock star, Bob Geldof, organized Live Aid, a concert that raised millions of dollars for Ethiopia. U2 played in the concert, and Bono and his wife, Alison, later traveled to Africa. Bono came to understand that onerous debt-service obligations dwarfed the charitable contributions Live Aid had mobilized. Bono got involved in advocacy and found Jamie Drummond to be his advisor.

In 2004 Bread for the World organized services of prayer for poor people at the Democratic and Republican national conventions. Bono came to the Republican event. He arrived late, as usual, but after he spoke he sat down next to me and sang hymns with us. He and I were sitting next to an open door behind the pulpit of the church. His handler kept poking her head around the corner, urging Bono to leave for his next gig. But Bono was enjoying the worship and stayed to listen to my sermon. He told the gathering, "David Beckmann is my rock star." My son Andrew, then a college student, was at the service but wasn't convinced that his father was a rock star.

Bono proposed a campaign that would include Bread

for the World, other church groups, and major international charities that were becoming more involved in advocacy. Bread for the World invested heavily in helping Bono launch what became the ONE Campaign. The ONE Campaign has enlisted more than 2 million Americans in Web-based advocacy on global poverty issues and has now launched similar efforts in Europe and Japan.

I have worked with other celebrities, but Bono is exceptional. He visits Africa and studies the issues. When he meets with a senator, he is informed and convincing. I have come to trust his motives. Bono is also a poet. He writes song lyrics that are important to millions of people, and he also speaks about Africa in a gritty and inspiring way.

I've learned a lot from Bono and his advisors about mass media and the Web. The companies that contract with celebrities invest millions of dollars to build public excitement around them. Personally I'm not very interested in celebrities, but this public excitement is a valuable commodity. If Bono allows his image to appear on the home page of Google, that will draw business and make it profitable for Google to promote Bono's message about Africa. A stable of companies are marketing products in association with RED, a Bono brand that benefits the Global Fund for AIDS.

Bono has urged his celebrity friends to join him in advocacy for Africa. When Brad Pitt agreed to help the ONE Campaign, my longtime assistant Dolly Youssef laughed at me because I wrote on my to-do list: "Find out who Brad Pitt is."

I spoke to a group of conservative Baptist church leaders a few months later. Many people in the group were skeptical about any role for the U.S. government in reducing poverty. I mentioned some of the evangelical church leaders who work with Bread for the World. But that conservative crowd only warmed up when I mentioned Brad

Pitt. The room erupted in giggles, and I could feel that my message was suddenly getting through.

I met Brad Pitt and Angelina Jolie at President Clinton's annual conference on global issues. I told them about my experience with these Baptists. Brad laughed about the influence of celebrities in our culture. I was impressed that Brad Pitt and Angelina Jolie seemed intent on learning more about Africa. They wanted to use their influence in ways that would really help.

More than half of all U.S. press coverage of Africa in 2005 was driven by celebrities, including a trip that ABC news correspondent Diane Sawyer made to Africa with Pitt. Television journalists quoted celebrities about Africa fifteen times more often than they quoted Africans.[3]

When British Prime Minister Tony Blair hosted the G8 Summit in 2005, he focused the agenda on Africa. Bono and Bob Geldof decided to organize Live 8 concerts, an echo of the Live Aid concert a decade before but now focused on getting the G8 heads of governments to make ambitious commitments to Africa. They proposed simultaneous concerts in all the G8 countries and South Africa. AOL agreed to broadcast the concerts for free, and top bands from all over the world agreed to appear.

I worked the press tent at the Live 8 concert in Philadelphia. Richard Branson, who owns Virgin Atlantic, provided an airplane to fly activists from Philadelphia to the summit site in Gleneagles, Scotland. Bread for the World organized the delegation of grassroots activists and church leaders that went to Scotland.

Jim Wallis, who heads the Christian social-justice organization Sojourners, organized a delegation of U.S. church leaders. We started with a meeting at the White House and then flew to London. Together with British and African church leaders, we met with Gordon Brown, then chancellor of the exchequer. We thanked the U.S. and U.K.

governments for focusing the G8 on global poverty and encouraged specific and ambitious agreements.

Live 8 made that year's G8 Summit a big media event. The G8 heads of government committed to doubling development aid to Africa and the rest of the developing world, and aid levels have increased since then. The G8 also committed to negotiating trade policies that would open opportunities for Africa and the rest of the developing world. That's a promise yet to be fulfilled.

If Bono had called for increases in U.S. development assistance ten years earlier, he would have failed. But public opinion in the United States and other industrialized countries had become more favorable toward helping Africa. The terrorist attacks of 2001 helped convince people that it's not smart to neglect misery in far-off places. Bono called for increasing aid to Africa at a time when many voters and political leaders thought it was the right thing to do. He made himself the spokesperson for a global grassroots movement.

Celebrities are gods in our society, and I am profoundly grateful to Bono and other celebrities for their powerful advocacy on behalf of Africa and poor people around the world.

Bill Gates and Other Wealthy Allies

My strangest meeting with Bono was in New York in the fall of 2002. Jamie Drummond shot me a quick e-mail to say that he and Bono were going to meet for drinks with some people from the Gates Foundation that Friday evening. Could I join them? I didn't hear from Jamie again, but I got on the train from Washington to New York, not sure that I'd find anybody at the restaurant.

When I arrived, people were gathering at a huge oval table in a private dining room. Over the course of the evening, more people joined us—Trevor Neilson and Joe Cerrell from the Gates Foundation, Bobby Shriver and a couple of his friends, the person in charge of marketing for U2, colleagues from the U.S. Conference of Catholic Bishops and the Episcopal Church, and a reporter from *Time* magazine (who soon after wrote a cover article titled "Can Bono Save the World?").

We talked about how to strengthen U.S. political support for progress against global poverty. Bono and Bill Gates had spoken on a conference panel together that afternoon, and we expected that Bono might join our conversation. The discussion went through dinner and into the night. Finally, sometime after 1 a.m., Jamie received a call: "B" was on his way. I guess rock stars don't keep the same schedule as preachers. Bono finally arrived at about 2 a.m., and that's when I figured out what the meeting was about. He was trying to convince Bill Gates and his foundation to support advocacy for Africa. He argued that the Jubilee mix of celebrity power with grassroots, faith-based advocacy could sway U.S. policy.

The story of Bill and Melinda Gates's involvement in global health is stunning in itself. They were considering ways to "give back" some of the billions of dollars Bill had made at Microsoft when they read an article on an obscure disease called rotavirus. It was eliminated long ago in this country, but was killing half a million children a year in the developing world. They couldn't believe such a plague had not received the modest funding needed to make the cure available in poor countries.[4]

That started Bill and Melinda's transformational involvement in global health. They established the Gates Foundation in 2000 and focused their early grants on vaccines that could have a big impact among poor people around the world.

Initially, they had no interest in public-policy advocacy. They had lots of money; why get involved with government? But the couple soon figured out that U.S. government funding and policies are crucial to the gains in global health they want to achieve. Bono's conversations with them about advocacy helped make the case. The Gates Foundation ultimately provided substantial support for the ONE Campaign, Bread for the World Institute, and other advocacy groups.

In 2006 I received another cryptic e-mail. Patty Stonesifer, the CEO of the Gates Foundation, invited me to a meeting with Bill and Melinda at the New York Public Library the following Monday. It turned out to be the event at which investor Warren Buffett gave $31 billion to the Gates Foundation. The gift was made simply, without much fanfare. Buffett handed Bill Gates what appeared to be a short, signed contract. When Bill Gates passed it on to someone on the foundation staff, he just smiled and said, "Don't lose that."

I thanked Buffett and Bill and Melinda Gates for their extraordinary generosity. I said that their example is even more important than their money. Lots of Americans used to think that investing in poor people was throwing money down a rat hole. It's hard to maintain that cynicism when the world's most successful entrepreneur and investor both invest in poor people.

I had already been in touch with several of the Buffett family members. My wife grew up in Omaha, Nebraska, a few blocks from the modest home where the Buffetts lived for many years. I sent an e-mail about Buffett's gift to his grandson Howie, who was starting graduate school. It would have been understandable if family members preferred that some of those Buffett billions remain in his estate for them, but Howie wrote back, "This has been the proudest day of my life."

A growing number of other wealthy people have become involved in the cause of global poverty, often including advocacy. These philanthropists are part of a broader trend in U.S. giving. Public giving to U.S. charities that help poor people overseas has expanded, and the importance of advocacy is now widely understood. When I talked about advocacy in the 1990s, people often reacted quizzically. Today more people understand that advocacy should be part of our response to poverty.

Movement among People of Faith

At Bread for the World, we are especially thrilled that new doors have opened among Christians of all varieties, Jews, and Muslims.

Historically, evangelical Protestant leaders discouraged church involvement in politics. But evangelicals became more involved in politics in recent decades, partly because political conservatives organized in evangelical churches. Jerry Falwell, a television preacher, founded the Moral Majority in 1979. He encouraged many conservative Christians to register to vote and get involved in politics. Pat Robertson and Ralph Reed founded the Christian Coalition in 1987. The Christian Coalition organized conservative Christians to make themselves influential in the local committees of the Republican Party, and they distributed 40 million election guides in 1994, mainly at churches. Conservative Christian voters contributed to the growing strength of the Republican Party in the 1990s.

Some conservative activists and the press exaggerated

the extent to which organizations like the Christian Coalition represented all evangelicals, and many evangelicals became uncomfortable with how they were being portrayed in the media. Evangelical leaders such as Ron Sider, Jim Wallis, Glenn Palmberg, and Daniel Vestal helped evangelicals see the connections between biblical faith and justice for poor people. Evangelical denominations such as the Christian Reformed Church, the Evangelical Covenant Church, and the Cooperative Baptist Fellowship have become very active in promoting advocacy for hungry and poor people.

Rick Warren is the pastor of Saddleback Church, a California megachurch, the leader of a network of churches across the country, and author of a best-selling book, *The Purpose-Driven Life*. His wife, Kay, was gripped by an article she read about AIDS, and she and Rick later traveled to Rwanda. They were led by the Spirit to a much more active concern about poverty, especially global AIDS. This "second conversion" made Rick a credible representative of a broad cross section of the religious community in the presidential campaign of 2008. The two candidates agreed to have him do back-to-back interviews with them on national television.

Bill Hybels is the pastor of another influential megacongregation, Willow Creek Community Church in South Barrington, Illinois. He and his wife, Lynne, have experienced a similar awakening, and, like the Warrens, understand that faithful discipleship should include advocacy. They have focused especially on global AIDS and world hunger. They have also reached out to people in need and diverse ethnic groups in their own community.

The AIDS epidemic in Africa engaged many evangelicals in advocacy for poor people. World Vision, an international development agency with many evangelical donors, surveyed evangelical churchgoers in 2001 and found that they didn't want to help people with AIDS. Many thought AIDS was divine punishment for promiscuity.[5] But the leaders of World Vision, to their great credit, decided to make AIDS their organization's top priority anyway.

Franklin Graham (the son of Billy Graham) convened a Washington conference on AIDS, and Senator Jesse Helms agreed to speak. President Bush's White House was in close touch with conservative evangelical leaders, and some of these leaders used their access to argue for a response to AIDS in Africa. Michael Gerson, an evangelical who was President Bush's speechwriter, made the case for a presidential AIDS initiative from within the White House. The international AIDS program that President Bush launched has reached 2.4 million people with life-saving medicines and another 29 million people with testing and counseling about HIV and AIDS.[6]

Many people in the current generation of college students and young adults are eager to become involved in social change, including advocacy for poor people, and this is also true among young evangelicals. One reason is that many church colleges now send their students abroad. Also, many young evangelicals are discovering what the Bible teaches about social justice. When I talk about the Bible and poverty at evangelical colleges and seminaries, students often come up to me afterward to say that they want to commit their lives to justice for hungry and poor people.

GYUDE MOORE

Gyude Moore, now thirty years old, grew up in Liberia (in West Africa) and came to the United States for college. He is living out a promise he made as a teenager.

Gyude (pronounced JOO-day) was one of seven children of a government official. The family was relatively well-off, the children went to a Catholic school, and they even owned a car—an early-model Mitsubishi Lancer.

When Gyude was fourteen, civil war broke out in Liberia. Because of his father's position, Gyude's family was a target for the rebels and had to flee repeatedly to Ivory Coast. Each time, they had to walk thirty miles to a refugee camp on the other side of the border.

When Gyude was sixteen, his mother gave birth to twins—a boy and a girl. Shortly after, the violence got worse again, and the Moores had to make the trek to Ivory Coast. Gyude carried his baby brother, named Blo (which means "earth"). His mother carried the baby girl, but she was too frail to make the trip. Before the family reached the border, the baby girl died.

Gyude's voice still breaks as he describes his mother's grief and his own powerlessness. His mother didn't cry until late that evening in the camp. She tried to muffle the sounds of her grief so she wouldn't wake the other children. But Gyude heard her.

That is when he made his promise. He swore—to himself, to his mother, to God—that if he survived the war, he would grow up to be a "big man" (the term used to describe an important leader in Liberia). But he wouldn't work for social status or wealth just for himself and his family. Instead, he would fight the causes of poverty and war, the conditions that led to his sister's death and his mother's suffering.

Gyude believes that God has taken him up on that promise. He finished high school in Ivory Coast. At some point he saw a brochure about Berea College in far-off Kentucky. But Gyude was involved with a group of charismatic Christians and was "on fire for Jesus," and he enrolled in a Baptist seminary back in Liberia. He studied there for three years and planned to pastor a church, until nearby fighting forced him to quit seminary.

Gyude remembers going out on his back porch on a very dark night to pray. He told God he was trying to make good on his promise, but didn't know what to do if he couldn't finish seminary. In the dark of the night, he remembered Berea. It was an answer to prayer.

When he went inside, he told his younger brothers that one year from that date he would be studying in the United States. They laughed at him, but the next day he went to a store and bought a suitcase. Gyude filled out an online application to Berea College, and they accepted him. On the day he applied for a visa, only two of forty-one applicants received visas. It all seems miraculous to Gyude.

As a student at Berea, Gyude joined an Oxfam America training program for young leaders of activism against global poverty. In 2003 he invited me to speak at an event he organized. He had single-handedly recruited more than three hundred students from colleges throughout the southeastern United States.

The most moving moment of the event was when Gyude stood up during a "hunger banquet." Students were asked to read descriptions of the evening meals of hungry people in different parts of the world, but Gyude put down his paper and said, "There is really no point for me to read this made-up description. Not long ago, I was this hungry person. The night before I went to apply for my visa to the United States, all we had in the house to eat was rice. My brother was cooking it, and he was a horrible cook. He burnt it, so he had to keep adding water to make it edible. It never really was edible—just burnt rice with so much water that it became soup. But we ate it, because that was all we had."

After college, Gyude joined Bread for the World's staff as a grassroots organizer. He recalls his first visit to Capitol Hill. He specifically remembers the echo of his brown shoes as he walked the marble halls of a Senate office building: "I realized that when I was in Africa, I accepted things that happened to me like I accepted the weather. But suddenly I was here, talking to some of the most powerful people in the world, trying to influence the economic policy of the most powerful nation in the world. In that moment I went from powerless to powerful. Often, U.S. policy has a greater influence on us in Africa than we have ourselves."

Gyude left Bread's staff to pursue a graduate degree in foreign affairs at Georgetown University. His focus of study was fragile states. He was also elected to the board of Bread for the World.

Gyude is still dealing with serious family problems. After he left for the United States, his little brother Blo joined the rebels in Liberia. Gyude felt guilty, saying that Blo always lived in his shadow and joined the rebels because he wanted to be good at something. Like many other rebels in Liberia, Blo became addicted to heroin. Through IV drug use he contracted HIV/AIDS and ultimately died from the disease.

Gyude's income at Georgetown was his fifteen-thousand-dollar annual stipend. But he stretched it to help support a baby daughter, Ade, and send money back to family in Liberia. It was vastly more than anyone in his family back home earns. Many members of Gyude's family wanted him to stay in the United States. "When I was admitted to the United States, many people in my family saw it as their redemption," he says.

But Gyude has returned to Liberia to serve on the staff of President Ellen Johnson-Sirleaf, the first woman head of state in Africa. He helps to write some of her speeches. After his years in the United States, he's struck by how few Liberians are well-educated—and by how challenging it is for the senior people around him to govern the country well. He is tracking two projects for the president—the airport and low-income housing estates.

Since 2006, top leaders from all the families of U.S. Christianity have been meeting once a year. Their loose association, Christian Churches Together (CCT), is the most inclusive organization of Christian bodies in U.S. history, and their main topic of conversation has been poverty in America. The group includes Catholics, Orthodox, historic Protestants (such as Methodists and Presbyterians), evangelical and pentecostal Protestants, African American churches, and interdenominational organizations such as Bread for the World.

The evangelical Protestant leaders were the ones to propose that the early CCT discussions focus on U.S. poverty. Whether Protestant or Catholic, liberal or conservative, many church leaders have become convinced that our nation and its churches are doing less than we should to deal with poverty in our communities.

In the past, there were sharp division between churches that emphasized evangelism and others that emphasized justice for poor people. But the CCT discussions suggest this division may be fading. The CCT leaders agree that churches must be about sharing the gospel of Jesus Christ, and also that conversion must lead to helping poor people, including advocacy. These leaders have spoken out together about domestic poverty issues to the press and to White House officials.

At the CCT meeting in 2010, Bread for the World reported on how churches have responded to the increase in poverty caused by recession. During the financial crisis year of 2008, charities in general suffered a decline in giving, but religious congregations and food banks both reported increases in giving. Many denominations and local churches, across all the varieties of Christianity in the United States, increased assistance to people in need in their communities.[7]

Latino churches are likely to be a growing force in

advocacy for poor people. One of my proudest achievements was preaching in Spanish at Templo Calvario, an Assemblies of God megachurch in Orange County, California. About five thousand people, mostly under age thirty, worship at Templo Calvario every Sunday. I can speak decent Spanish, but a pentecostal congregation expects a preacher to be spontaneous and to pick up speed toward the end of the sermon. I did pretty well for a Lutheran, and the good people at Templo Calvario were tolerant. They even appreciated my efforts to dance a bit during their praise songs.

Their pastor, Daniel de Leon, added a little sermon of his own to my sermon, and his words made it clear why Latino churches of all stripes are open to involvement in advocacy on hunger-related issues. "Hunger is something we know," Daniel said. "Please stand up if you have ever had to go without food." About a third of the congregation stood up. "We're going to take up a collection for Bread for the World now. But this is for hungry people, so if you don't have enough food at home, take five or ten dollars out of the plate."

The people of Templo Calvario contributed enough to provide for some immediate needs and sent me away with sixteen thousand dollars for Bread for the World.

Jewish and Muslim groups have also become more involved in advocacy for hungry and poor people, often working together with Christian groups. Over the past few years, Bread and the Alliance to End Hunger have helped MAZON ("mazon" is the Hebrew word for food) and American Jewish World Service develop education and advocacy materials on hunger. The Jewish Council on Public Affairs has become active in changing the politics of hunger and poverty in America. Bread and the Alliance have also worked with Muslim leaders. We have helped develop materials that go out annually to more than five hundred thousand U.S. Muslims to encourage help and advocacy for hungry people during Ramadan.

Bread for the World has organized two big interfaith convocations on hunger at the Washington National Cathedral. Seldom in U.S. history has the top leadership of such a diverse array of religious leaders come together, and thousands of people participated. These interfaith events grew out of a suggestion from MAZON. Muslim groups have been eager to join with Christians and Jews against hunger, partly as a way to counter the suspicion and discrimination U.S. Muslims have suffered since the 2001 terrorist attacks. African American, Latino, and Native American religious leaders have participated; so have Buddhists and Sikhs. These convocations have been a significant religious experience for some of the religious leaders themselves.

Meanwhile, the Democratic Party has been working to improve its connections with the religious community, focusing on religious concern about poverty. The majority of the people who go to religious services regularly vote Republican, and Christian conservatives have organized themselves as a force within the Republican Party. But after the Republican sweep of 2004, many Democratic politicians took to expressing their faith and talking about God and poverty. Changes in the voting patterns of churchgoers contributed to the election of President Obama and a Democratic majority in Congress in 2008.

Clinton, Bush, and Obama

Our last three presidents have all provided some leadership on poverty issues. President Clinton managed to reduce poverty in the United States, thanks mainly to good macroeconomic management and his expansion of the Earned

Income Tax Credit. Toward the end of his time in the White House he focused on global poverty, which has become a driving passion for him at the Clinton Foundation.

When George W. Bush was running for president, he said we should focus on those parts of the world in which the United States has interests. He then listed all the regions of the world except Africa. Nobody expected him to propose major new programs of foreign aid. Yet U.S. aid to Africa quadrupled during the Bush administration.[8] The United States also offered African nations new openings for trade. President Bush did more for Africa than any U.S. president before him.

What accounts for his strong leadership on African issues? He is personally concerned, and he also came to see that freedom from disease and misery is related to his deep commitments to human freedom and national security. Bush's Africa policies also benefited from good advisors and strong support from members of Congress of both parties.

I had a chance to talk with President Bush during his last month in office. My wife and I are members of Christ Church in Alexandria, Virginia. George Washington was a member there, and many presidents have visited. When President and Mrs. Bush visited, I told him about some of the people I've met in Africa who are alive today only because of his push to get AIDS medicine to Africans. "It's been a labor of love," he said. He looked to the altar in the front of the church. "That's why we did it."

Domestic poverty has always been a higher political priority than global poverty. But while interest in global poverty surged during the Bush years, there was no comparable increase in political interest in domestic poverty. We still get no help from rock stars on issues that are important to poor people in the United States.

Yet our Alliance to End Hunger polls document strong

and growing concern among voters about domestic hunger and poverty. About three-quarters of voters favor spending additional tax dollars on federal hunger programs to end child hunger in the United States. Voters are aware that many people have been driven into poverty by the nation's economic problems, through no fault of their own.

When we discussed the Alliance's polling results with former president Bill Clinton, he said that the important question for a politician is what single issue will most determine the choice of voters. So in one poll we asked, "Thinking about the next time you vote for Congress or U.S. Senate, what one issue do you view as the most important to you in deciding your vote?" Top issues were health care, taxes, and the economy. But 7 percent of voters said the issue that would sway their vote would be hunger and poverty. That's more than opted for the environment or immigration. Most of the voters who said hunger or poverty is their decisive issue had relatively low incomes. Many were African American or Latino.

Measured by press coverage, poverty was discussed more than three times as much in the 2007–2008 presidential campaign as in the 2003–2004 campaign.[9] Then-senator Obama spoke much more about poverty than Senator McCain, and that helped Obama win the election. Obama proposed programs to end child hunger in this country by 2015 and to cut poverty in half within ten years. He also promised to help achieve the Millennium Development Goals, partly by doubling U.S. foreign aid and making it more effective.

But hunger and poverty were not leading campaign issues for either presidential candidate. Belmont University in Nashville hosted the second presidential debate. Belmont is a Christian university, and they invited me to preach at an ecumenical prayer service before the debate. I noted that there had been no mention of poverty in the first presidential debate: "The candidates have expressed so much concern about the middle class that I checked my Bible. I thought maybe the Lord must have said, 'Whatever you do for the struggling middle class, you've done it unto me.'" I stole that line from John Carr, who works for the U.S. Conference of Catholic Bishops, and repeated it in radio interviews that reached 20 million people. I was pleased when, during the last debate, Obama mentioned that his family relied on food stamps when he was a boy.

Since coming to power, President Obama has continued to talk about struggling Americans, and he has not abandoned his specific promises to hungry and poor people in this country and worldwide. In fact, his actions for poor people have been more ambitious than his rhetoric. President Obama's commitments open the door to expanded efforts to reduce hunger and poverty, but he cannot realize these promises without help in building congressional support among both Republicans and Democrats.

In our system, the president, more than anyone else, sets the nation's agenda of political discussion. When President Bush proposed strengthening development assistance, it made sense for advocates to support and shape the president's proposals. President Obama has made more ambitious commitments to hungry and poor people in the United States and worldwide, and it makes sense for advocates—whether Democrats, Republicans, or independents—to push the administration and Congress to shape those commitments into effective action.

CHAPTER 8

A TIME TO CHANGE
HISTORY FOR
HUNGRY PEOPLE

We are at a pivotal point in the history of poverty. Economic turmoil has driven many more people into hunger and poverty. But the clear need for national change, an increasingly significant movement against hunger and poverty, voter attitudes, and the commitments of our current president give us a political opening. We may be able to achieve policy changes that will help people in need and set a path toward ending hunger and poverty. At a minimum, faith-grounded activists can make the future better for hungry people than it would otherwise be.

This chapter outlines an agenda for policy change. It explains four issues that are important to hungry people and on which breakthroughs are possible. The chapter then discusses the hunger and poverty dimension of high-profile issues our nation is likely to be debating. The chapter ends with a section on what we need to do to seize the opportunity we now have to change history for hungry people.

Ending Child Hunger

During his campaign for election, President Obama promised to end child hunger in America by 2015 and cut U.S. poverty in half. The Obama campaign issued a solid plan to end child hunger. It rightly includes three elements: stronger national nutrition programs, more effective community efforts, and policies to reduce poverty. I want to hold him to those promises, translate them into effective programs, and help him secure the necessary support from Congress. There is a long tradition of bipartisanship in responding to hunger.

The federal government maintains three large nutrition programs. The largest is the Supplemental Nutrition Assistance Program (SNAP). It is complemented by the Women, Infants, and Children Program (WIC), which provides additional, appropriate food to infants, children, and their mothers. School Meals is the third area of nutrition assistance: school lunches, school breakfasts, after-school, and summer programs. Our national nutrition programs are effective instruments for reducing hunger, and we can go a long way toward ending child hunger by making the most of them.

Congress is updating policies regarding these programs. The administration has asked Congress for an additional $1 billion a year to get food to vulnerable children and fund improved nutrition in school lunches, and Bread for the World members are urging their members of Congress to help make this happen.

The Obama campaign statement on child hunger also talks about enhancing the impact of community efforts to help hungry people. More than sixty-three thousand charitable agencies provide food to hungry people.[1] They are on the front lines, meeting the needs of desperate people.

Most of these programs are small, and their funding is always a challenge.

But the many organizations that deal with hunger in a community can have a bigger impact if they cooperate and think strategically. They can figure out what needs to happen over a period of years to reduce and perhaps end hunger in their communities. The national nutrition programs aren't fully utilized (for example, only two-thirds of people eligible for SNAP apply), so community efforts can tap into available federal funding. Food charities can help people enroll in SNAP, insist that their local schools provide breakfast for low-income children, and organize summer feeding programs. Community leaders can also spot ways to coordinate federal, state, and community programs to take full advantage of available resources. When people who provide assistance have a chance to think together about systemic solutions, they almost always decide to expand and improve what they do to advocate for policy changes at the city, state, and national levels.

Bread and now the Alliance to End Hunger have helped many community coalitions against hunger. We also pushed Congress to approve the Hunger-Free Communities Program, which is now funding similar work on a larger scale.

The Obama campaign statement was also clear that ending child hunger won't be achieved by food assistance alone. We need complementary measures to reduce poverty, notably tax credits for poor working families. As a candidate, Obama supported tax credits and also outlined a broader strategy to cut poverty in half.

Bread for the World's 2010 Offering of Letters built popular support for tax credits that help low-income working families. These include the Earned Income Tax Credit, which boosts wages for the working poor, and the Child Tax Credit. These credits increase the refunds that low-income workers get on their tax returns. Tax credits are the government's largest antipoverty programs. The Earned Income Tax Credit alone lifts 7 million people — half of them children — out of poverty.[2]

As the political parties debate tax regulations, especially tax benefits for affluent people, advocates for hungry children need to rally around these tax provisions that help poor working families. Bread for the World has repeatedly invited churches across the country to help us strengthen the national nutrition programs, and church people also need to understand that better wages for low-income workers are important to hungry children.

We want President Obama to be explicit about his continuing commitment to the goal of ending child hunger. His rhetoric about the struggling middle class may have broader political appeal. But a big majority of U.S. voters say we should try to end child hunger in this country, and we aren't going to achieve that goal unless the president is explicit about what we are trying to do. Michelle Obama is encouraging good nutrition for children, and we would like her to be more forceful in talking about children who don't get enough to eat.

We urgently need to moderate child hunger in this time of high unemployment. Once the economy expands again, we could make rapid strides toward ending child hunger in America.

The Global Hunger and Food Security Initiative

President Obama made this promise in his inaugural address: "To the people of poor nations, we pledge to work alongside you to make your farms flourish and let clean waters flow; to nourish starved bodies and feed hungry minds."

I was thrilled—but even more thrilled when the president and Secretary of State Hillary Clinton later announced they were indeed launching a global hunger and food security initiative. Bread for the World immediately convened a coalition to help shape and support it. By the second year of the administration, Congress had doubled U.S. funding for agricultural development assistance, and the administration was proposing further increases.

An increase in aid to develop agriculture in poor countries is long overdue. Developing-country governments have underinvested in agriculture, mainly because people in urban areas tend to be stronger politically. International aid agencies have also underinvested in agriculture. Rural roads have been neglected, for example. Fertilizer prices are high, and the prices farmers get for their crops are low, because it is expensive—or impossible—to run trucks into many parts of rural Africa.

Grain prices have moderated since they spiked in 2008, but they are expected to remain high relative to recent decades. High grain prices have increased hunger among poor consumers, but also opened new opportunities for investment in agriculture. Many of the poorest people in the world are farmers. With quality seeds, fertilizers, and better rural roads, poor farmers can increase their production, raise their own incomes, and help moderate prices for poor people who have to buy food.

The U.S. world hunger initiative, called Feed the Future, is investing in the agricultural productivity of poor farmers. Our government is responding to plans developed by poor-country governments. U.S. officials are also promoting consultations with farmers' associations, women's groups, and religious bodies to help make the initiative responsive to local realities and encourage coordination among all the actors involved.

Partly in response to Bread for the World advocacy,

the U.S. initiative includes a specific focus on undernourished children. A major international study of nutrition programs published in *The Lancet*, a British medical journal, in 2008 has given us new clarity about what interventions are most effective in reducing death and disease due to undernutrition. The lessons are these: focus on babies and pregnant women, promote healthy family habits (such as breast-feeding and hand washing), get special foods to severely undernourished children, and add a few key vitamins and minerals to foods that everybody eats (iodine in salt, for example, and Vitamin A in cooking oil).

Rather than go it alone, the United States is also encouraging other governments and the private sector to ramp up their investment in poor-country agriculture. At his first G8 Summit in July 2009, President Obama convinced the other major industrial countries to promise major increases in their assistance to poor-country agriculture. I attended a heartening meeting at the United Nations in September 2009, cochaired by Secretary Clinton and U.N. Secretary General Ban Ki-moon. The leaders of many nations talked about their participation in this global mobilization to strengthen food security and reduce world hunger. It was great to see our government using its international influence for good.

In April 2010 I attended a prayer breakfast at the White House and spoke briefly with President Obama. I thanked him for the commitments he has made to hungry and poor people in our country and worldwide. He replied, "We're serious about the global food security initiative, and we intend to mobilize serious money behind it." The United States has never before led an international effort to reduce world hunger.

This U.S.-led effort to reduce world hunger will require sustained attention from concerned citizens. We must insist that Congress funds it, and legislation may be needed to make it a long-term, bipartisan commitment. We will also need to monitor that the initiative is effectively administered.

NORMAN BORLAUG

Norman Borlaug won a Nobel Prize in 1970 for his contribution to the Green Revolution of Asia. As an agricultural researcher he helped develop high-yielding varieties of wheat. He then played a driving role in getting Pakistan, India, and most other Asian countries to promote new varieties of wheat and rice among their farmers.

In the 1960s South Asia suffered famines, and many experts predicted mass starvation. The new varieties dramatically increased food production, raised the incomes of poor farmers, and reduced prices for poor consumers. The Green Revolution ended famines in South Asia. In retrospect, not enough was done to include very poor farmers or protect the environment, but the Green Revolution was nevertheless a huge success.

Borlaug was seventy years old when a Japanese philanthropist, Ryoichi Sasakawa, telephoned in 1984. Sasakawa was funding humanitarian aid in response to Ethiopia's famine, but called to ask Borlaug to help foster a Green Revolution in Africa. With Sasakawa's support, Norman Borlaug worked for another twenty-five years to reduce hunger in Africa. He helped Ethiopia and several other African countries raise agricultural productivity.

I recommend a remarkable book about Dr. Borlaug and world hunger, *Enough*, by Roger Thurow and Scott Kilman, longtime reporters at the *Wall Street Journal*. After writing the book, Roger decided to leave his job at the *Journal* to devote himself full-time to building the constituency needed to end world hunger.

When Borlaug was in his mid-nineties he got very sick,

and his family and associates started to plan for his eventual memorial service. They asked me to serve as the clergyman. I flew to Dallas to talk with Dr. Borlaug about it. When I asked what hymns he would want us to sing, he was adamant about the "Iowa Corn Song"—not great music by any means, but he sang it every morning as an Iowa schoolboy, and it expressed his devotion to agriculture.

I have never met anyone who was more committed to a cause than Norman Borlaug. A couple of days before his death, he was half-sleeping but became agitated. His daughter asked him, "Daddy, is something bothering you?"

"I have a problem," he replied.

His daughter was eager to help him rest comfortably. "What's your problem?" she asked.

"Africa," said Dr. Borlaug. On his deathbed, he was thinking about his unfinished work for a Green Revolution in Africa. By coincidence, Secretary of State Hillary Clinton outlined the U.S. global hunger and food security initiative just one month before Norman Borlaug's death.

On Borlaug's last day, a researcher from Oklahoma State visited to explain a new technology that could help African farmers fertilize their crops. Dr. Borlaug eyes were closed, but he listened.

"Get it to the farmers," he said. Those were his last words.

More and Better Development Assistance

President Obama also wants the United States to support achievement of the Millennium Development Goals. He has promised to double development assistance (adding $25 billion) and create a transformed development aid agency.

Because of alarm about the U.S. fiscal deficit, Congress won't approve continuing increases in development assistance unless some of their constituents insist on it. Poor people themselves and the governments of poor countries will continue to provide most of the resources needed for their development. Yet aid from the United States and other industrialized countries is an important supplement, especially now, when most developing countries are struggling with global economic problems.

Development assistance should be focused on moving forward toward the Millennium Development Goals. As 2015 approaches, the United States should also provide leadership for international agreement on an updated version of the Millennium Goals—perhaps looking forward to 2025.

At the international climate-change summit in 2009 the United States offered to provide substantial additional assistance to help developing countries do their part to slow climate change (reducing pollution and protecting tropical forests) and to deal with its impact. Climate change is already causing droughts: the International Panel on Climate Change estimates that 75 to 250 million Africans will be exposed to increased water stress by 2020. Less water will be available in the heavily populated river basins of Asia by 2050. In coastal areas, resources are needed to deal with increased flooding. Climate change further adds to the need for investment in agriculture. Without investments to help farmers adapt, yields from rain-fed agriculture in some African countries will drop by half by 2020.[3]

Bread for the World is also engaged in a major, multiyear campaign to reform U.S. foreign assistance. We want to make sure that aid dollars are used well, and that more of our aid gets to people who really need help. I cochair a coalition of think tanks, advocacy groups, and charities that work in developing countries. It is called the Modernizing

Foreign Assistance Network. The Hewlett Foundation has provided important support for this cause.

Bread for the World and our coalition partners have urged that the United States put more emphasis in its foreign policy on poverty reduction and development. The Obama administration has indeed put more emphasis on development, but U.S. diplomatic and military purposes still too often compromise development programs. Such compromise is clear from the distribution of U.S. assistance to developing countries. Most U.S. aid goes to Iraq, Afghanistan, Egypt, Colombia, Jordan, Ethiopia, and Nigeria—all countries that are important to U.S. interests. Other developing countries get tiny slivers of the aid pie.[4]

Figure 7   **Distribution of U.S. Aid by Country, 2004–2008**

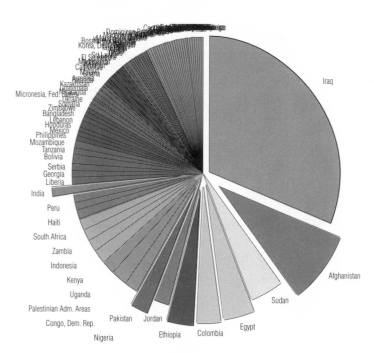

Source: William Easterly and Laura Freschi, based on data from the Organization for Economic Cooperation and Development.

Bread for the World wants to see resources shifted to poverty-focused development assistance, which doesn't include most of the U.S. aid that goes to Afghanistan and Iraq or other politically motivated aid. In other ways, too, we want our government to put more emphasis on development, especially the reduction of poverty.

Bread for the World and its coalition are also pushing for a strong international development agency within the U.S. government. At present, twelve departments, twenty-five different agencies, and nearly sixty government offices maintain foreign assistance programs. The U.S. Agency for International Development (USAID), our government's lead development agency, needs to be revitalized. It should focus on development, with some separation from the diplomatic goals of the State Department. USAID's administrator should be invited into the highest councils of government, a voice for hungry and poor people around the world when our government is thinking about other issues, such as trade. Over time, other U.S. aid programs should be combined with USAID into one strong agency.

U.S. assistance should be more responsive to local situations and priorities. Our aid programs are now riddled with a host of competing objectives and earmarks, each of them responsive to some interest in the United States. Members of Congress lobby for earmarks for universities or businesses in their home districts, and charities lobby to get money for the sectors in which they work. Grassroots campaigns mobilize around particular diseases or causes. Congress and the president need to agree on a handful of priority goals, and detailed programs should be worked out on the ground in consultation with the host government and local communities.

Periodically, Congress "reauthorizes" programs in each area of government. The domestic child nutrition programs are normally reauthorized every five years, for example. At that time, Congress rethinks these programs and sets policies for the next five years. But our foreign aid programs have not gone through a comprehensive reauthorization for decades. The Foreign Assistance Act of 1961 — passed during the Kennedy administration — is still in effect.

Although President Obama and Secretary Clinton agree with most of these ideas about how to make foreign assistance more effective, their administration didn't initially want to use their limited political capital on foreign aid reform. When they came to power, they faced a host of other challenges. So Bread for the World's members and churches, together with our coalition partners, rallied around legislation in Congress that started the process. In response, the White House and State Department launched major processes to rethink foreign aid. They also began to implement these ideas as they launched their Feed the Future initiative, for example, and in response to the earthquake in Haiti.

But what's really needed is a comprehensive, bipartisan reauthorization of the Foreign Assistance Act. In that process the president and Congress would agree on the leading purposes of U.S. foreign assistance and revamp institutions and programs to serve those purposes.

Tessa Pulaski

In 2009 Bread for the World and many other groups pushed to get Congress and the president to start working on making foreign aid more effective. The new administration was preoccupied with lots of other problems. Representative Howard Berman, chair of the House Foreign Affairs Committee, was developing reform legislation. But Senator John Kerry, chair of the Senate Foreign Relations

Committee, was not sure that this issue had enough political support to get much done. Should the committee spend its time on reforming foreign aid if this effort wouldn't result in any real change?

Tessa Pulaski, a student at Sacred Heart High School in the Boston area, helped win him over. Tessa organized a Bread for the World club at her school. About thirty girls meet every two weeks to study hunger issues and write letters to their members of Congress. They wrote many letters to Senator Kerry about foreign assistance reform. Tessa joined a group of adult Bread for the World leaders in a visit to Kerry's Boston office. She and five friends then traveled to Washington. The girls had done their homework, and staff of the Senate Foreign Relations Committee met with them for over an hour.

When Kerry announced that he planned to introduce foreign aid reform legislation, he noted the importance of grassroots support. "As Congress and the administration have responded to people like us," says Tessa, "we have seen democracy in action."

Tessa and her group are now reaching out to engage other Sacred Heart schools across the country in advocacy. Tessa also recently landed an internship in Kerry's Boston office, and she is planning to spend next year in Latin America.

The Next Farm Bill

U.S. food and farm policies still cry out for broad reform. We spend billions of dollars on protectionist subsidies to affluent landowners. Those subsidies bypass the needs of farm and rural families who really need help. They stimulate agricultural production that is environmentally damaging, subsidized corn ethanol is an inefficient source of energy, and our farm policies often harm poor farmers and hungry people in poor countries. Americans and, increasingly, the rest of the world are struggling with an obesity epidemic. At the same time, hunger is widespread and has recently increased in our country and around the world.

To keep up with growing demand, global agricultural production needs to increase by about 50 percent by 2050.[5] Yet agriculture is less dynamic and responsive than it could be, because nearly all the world's countries maintain high tariffs and subsidies to protect their farms from agricultural imports.

The system is as bad as it is partly because the agriculture committees in the House and Senate are heavily influenced by interests that benefit from it. When the Farm Bill is reauthorized again, we will have another opportunity to push for reform. If the reform of U.S. farm policies is coupled with international leadership to reduce agricultural protectionism around the world, virtually all U.S. farmers stand to gain.

The Farm Bill includes the U.S. food aid programs, and they also need reform. The current rules stipulate that nearly all food aid has to travel on ships registered in the United States. This benefits a handful of shipping companies that are well organized in lobbying the agriculture committees. More than half of our food-aid dollars now fund transportation and administration. Allowing for the purchase of food closer to where it is needed would, in many cases, mean more and faster help to hungry people. It's hard to manage imported food aid in ways that don't depress the market for local farmers in poor countries, while buying food locally would boost the market for local farmers.

High-Profile Issues
and Poor People

Bread for the World plans to focus over the next few years on these four issues: ending child hunger in America, supporting and shaping the U.S. world hunger initiative, more and better development assistance, and Farm Bill reform. Success on these four issues would indeed change history for hungry people.

But our political leaders will be focused mainly on other issues that affect the country as a whole and seem more important to the media and most voters. The high-profile issues of the next few years will include the economy, the wars in Afghanistan and Iraq, health and education, energy, trade, and immigration. These issues affect the whole country, but advocates should call attention to how they affect poor people in particular. Each of these issues is multifaceted and controversial, so you probably won't agree with everything I say in this section. But I hope you will agree on the main point—that we and our political leaders need to keep poor and hungry people in mind as we deal with big issues like these.

The economy is a top national priority for lots of reasons, but a strong economy is urgently important to poor people. No country has achieved dramatic progress against poverty without sustained economic growth, and no feasible expansion of government antipoverty programs would do as much to help poor people as would a strong economy.

Stimulus spending by the government makes sense as long as demand is slack and many workers are unemployed. We cannot maintain today's level of deficit spending indefinitely; that would lead to financial crisis and widespread hardship, also among poor people. But as we balance different economic goals, macroeconomic policies that reduce unemployment are more important to poor people than any other government action.

Economic growth will also raise tax revenues and thus reduce deficit spending. But good fiscal management will also require higher tax rates for high- and middle-income people. Despite loud complaints about the oppressive tax burden, taxes are lower in the United States than in the other economically advanced countries, and the total tax burden on Americans is lower now than at any time since the 1950s.[6]

On the spending side, we devote one-fifth of the federal budget to each of three items—defense, Social Security, and health care—and we will need to cut expenses in these three big-ticket areas. We can reduce military spending and still be secure. We will also need to trim Social Security and Medicare benefits for upper- and middle-income people.

Few politicians dare to talk about raising taxes—or about cutting military expenses, Social Security, and Medicare—but as voters we must encourage them to provide serious strategies to reduce deficit spending.

Some politicians will use the deficit as an argument for cutting assistance to needy people. Yet all the programs of assistance for people facing hardship amount to only 14 percent of government spending. This includes tax credits for low-income workers; unemployment and disability insurance; and food stamps, school meals, and housing assistance.[7] We should insist on efficiency and results from these programs, but they can and should be protected from cuts.

Bread for the World argued for delay when the United States was considering the invasion of Iraq in 2003. Bread for the World always focuses on hunger; we don't pretend to speak with authority on issues of war and peace. But as an antihunger organization, we could see that the war would command massive resources and attention that might otherwise be devoted to reducing poverty. We knew that the war would also cause great hardship among people in Iraq. In retrospect, the financial and human costs of the wars in Iraq and Afghanistan have outweighed any benefits in terms of U.S. security or the well-being of people in these two countries. As our nation tries to find its way to an orderly, relatively positive end to these two wars, we should be keenly aware of all the good we could be doing with the $190 billion we are spending in Iraq and Afghanistan each year.

Health-care reform will continue to be a high-profile political issue. The 46 million people who now lack health insurance are mainly just above the poverty line and thus can't qualify for Medicaid, and health insurance will help many of these people stay out of poverty. A high priority going forward must be to reduce the gross inefficiencies in our health-care system—to improve our health, reduce the government's deficit spending, and make our economy more efficient.

Our educational system can also be improved, especially for young people from low-income families, and this may be a high-profile issue on which Republicans and Democrats can work together. Head Start, improved schools in low-income communities, and expanded community colleges are especially important to poor people.

As the president and Congress debate policies for energy independence and to combat global warming, we must again flag the interests of poor people. Poor people in this country can benefit from "green jobs" (the jobs needed to weatherize energy-inefficient buildings, for example), but they would be hit hard by higher prices for gas and home heating. Poor countries need assistance to help finance their environmental protection efforts and to cope with the negative impacts of global warming. Malawi needs to restore tree cover lost to firewood, for example, and Bangladesh will need to invest in flood protection and resettlement. So if the United States adopts a carbon tax or cap-and-trade system, some of the revenue should go to programs that address these impacts among poor people here and abroad.

Trade is a hard sell to working people in this country, especially right now. But trade fosters economic efficiencies and growth. We need that. If the job market improves, and health-care reform delivers real benefits to working people, voters may be ready to consider mutually beneficial trade negotiations. A new multilateral trade agreement would be powerful tonic for the global economy, and it would likely focus on agriculture, which is especially important to many poor rural people in developing countries. Assistance to workers in this country who are adversely affected by trade would need to be part of the deal.

Immigration is yet another controversial issue that will require action, and it is certainly important to hungry and poor people. In fact, international migration is a powerful part of the movement to end hunger and poverty. Most migrants into the United States are able to improve their economic well-being, and the money they send to their families reduces poverty in their home communities.

We need to regularize the legal situation of undocumented immigrants in this country and, at the same time, rationalize the enforcement of immigration laws. We can also slow migration by supporting economic development in Mexico, Central America, and the Caribbean, and investment in jobs, health, and education for working Americans will make immigration less threatening. A renewed effort to curtail drug abuse in the United States, including both law enforcement and stronger drug treatment programs, would help get drug-related violence in

Mexico under control. Providing opportunity for Mexican youth would also diminish the lure of the drug trade.

All these high-profile issues are complex, and people of goodwill have various opinions about them. But as we wrestle with questions that affect the nation as a whole, advocates should urge solutions that help — or at least don't hurt — poor people.

It Depends on Us

If we can achieve progress on the four issues highlighted in this chapter and get attention to hunger and poverty in the big political debates of the next few years, it will have a huge impact for hungry and poor people.

But every point in this agenda will require major effort. People like us who care about hunger and poverty will need to push ferociously for change. This is not a time for advocacy as usual. This moment calls for smart strategy, sacrificial effort, and prayer.

Electoral politics are really important. We need to elect candidates who will support action to reduce hunger and poverty. They need our votes, volunteer time, and campaign contributions. Neither of the two major political parties is dominant, so each national election significantly changes the direction of the nation.

Bread for the World's network is campaigning on the issues highlighted in this chapter, and we are asking Bread's network of activists and churches to intensify their efforts. Bread for the World does more outright lobbying for poor people than any other organization in the country.

We are expanding what we do to get the word out about Bread for the World and making full use of Web-based communication. We are training young leaders and engaging more African American and Latino churches.

We are also asking some Bread for the World leaders and activist teams to step up to a new level of competence and responsibility.

Many allied organizations and networks are also at work. The lines of work that strike me as especially important include advocacy at the federal level, advocacy at the state and local levels, and helping Christians grow in faith.

I don't now see much evidence of a wave of activism that we can just join. What I do see is that the current economic and political environment gives us an opportunity for major social change, and I am asking the readers of this book to make themselves leaders of that needed change.

We can achieve a lot with a surge of activism over the next few years. But we will then need to keep pushing to sustain U.S. government attention to poverty. So we are called—by the love of God—to get involved in some new activities right now and also to be open to long-term commitments.

U.S. religious history has been marked by a series of revivals, starting with the Great Awakening of the 1730s. At these times, many people have been gripped by the gospel and drawn into a deeper relationship with God. Some of these revivals have also contributed to movements of social reform, and that's what we should be praying and working for now—a justice revival. We need many people—some people who go to church and some who don't—to open our lives more fully to the Spirit of God.

The constituency to reduce poverty is much broader than the Christian community, of course. We need increased effort from all kinds of people and from diverse organizations—charities, foundations, civil rights organizations, labor unions, corporations, and universities. We need leadership from political leaders and more attention to hunger and poverty within both political parties. Yet socially aware Christians have always helped to drive social-justice causes in the United States, and we won't achieve the progress against hunger and poverty that is possible unless some Christian believers feel called to make urgent and lasting adjustments in their lives.

> This is a pivotal point in the history of poverty. We are called to change the politics of hunger and poverty.

PART III

HOW WE GET THERE TOGETHER

CHAPTER 9

HOW GOD HAS DRAWN ME IN

God moves through history and shakes nations, but God also moves in the hearts and lives of individuals. I want to tell you how God has drawn me into the movement to overcome hunger and poverty.

Growing Up in Grace

My story started in a family where I always knew that my parents loved me — and lots of other people — and that their love came from God and Jesus.

I was shaped by unearned grace, which is also the main theme of my Lutheran tradition. Lutherans haven't always been strong in the area of social justice, but the emphasis on grace is a great resource. I experience a continual renewal, a continual sending out that comes from my baptism and from my ongoing experience of the grace of God in Jesus Christ. Every morning God says, "Okay, you're my child. You're you, could be better, but you're my child, and I have chosen you to go do this work today."

My mother and father grew up in rural Nebraska. My mother's father was a farmer, but became too ill to farm. She had to leave home at age sixteen, because her parents couldn't afford to feed her. She got a job as an elderly woman's helper in Lincoln, and she gave her parents much-needed furniture that first Christmas away from home. Mom never got to go to college.

Later in life, she taught sewing, paying particular attention to women who needed to sew to balance the family budget. When I was a teenager, she spent many hours studying the Bible and led a Bible study program at our church.

My father's dad was a small-town banker, but the bank went bankrupt during the Depression. My dad became a math teacher and then a school administrator. As a young superintendent of schools in small-town Nebraska during the Second World War, he faced down threats of violence to protect a Japanese American family.

He believed strongly in education, debate about ideas, and human rights for all people. By the time I was growing up, Dad was a professor of math education at the University of Nebraska at Lincoln. His primary focus was making sure that all children learned the basic math they needed to live in our society.

There were not extremes of wealth or poverty in Lincoln. It was a healthy community—although, in retrospect, some racial diversity would have livened things up.

Getting Started in the Sixties

I went to college at Yale University in the 1960s. That was during the Vietnam War and the movement to stop the war. I became convinced that the war was a mistake. I read critiques that viewed the Vietnam War as just one example of U.S. imperial power in the developing world.

William Sloane Coffin Jr. was Yale's chaplain, and my dorm room was just above his office. Coffin was a leader in the antiwar movement, and he made me more aware of what the Bible has to say about social justice. I sometimes attended a Lutheran church on the Hill, the African American neighborhood near Yale. The Black Power movement was at full strength then, and many African Americans were angry. That moment in American life gave me an abiding sense of the injustices in our country and the world.

When I graduated, Yale granted me a fellowship that allowed me to travel around the world and spend a year in Ghana. I spent fifty days in Asia and East Africa on the way to Ghana and fifty days in Europe on the way back.

In Ghana I studied indigenous pentecostal churches, the fastest-growing movement in African religion. These churches are thoroughly African—with dancing and drumming, visions and trances. When I went to Ghana I thought these churches were also politically progressive, but that turned out not to be the case. I learned to speak Twi, so I was able to spend time in villages and get to know people who didn't have much schooling. My first book, *Eden Revival*, was about indigenous African churches.

In my travels I focused on religion and politics—religion because of my upbringing, politics because of my experience at Yale. It was a moment of student unrest in most parts of the world, and I met with students in many of the countries I visited.

When I came back to the United States, I returned to Nebraska. Stokely Carmichael, a leader of the Black Power movement, had visited Yale and said to his audience of mainly white students, "Don't come to our communities to work. Go back to your own communities and change things there." That logic led me back to Nebraska.

I worked in various ways to "make the revolution" in Nebraska. You may not have noticed the lasting effects. I taught courses on social justice issues at a free school and a community college. I also traveled around the state, gaining some exposure to farmers, Indian reservations, and Nebraska's weak labor unions.

I also spent time with my parents, who were always interested in what I was learning. I made friends with the most radical students I could find in Nebraska. I also found Janet Williams, who became my wife in 1972.

My experience of teaching about justice quickly convinced me that lack of information was not the main obstacle. The persistence of injustice was rooted in spiritual problems. As a teenager I had thought I would become a pastor, and now I decided to go to seminary.

I attended Concordia Seminary in St. Louis, a seminary of the Lutheran Church—Missouri Synod, the conservative denomination in which I had been raised. Again following Stokely Carmichael's advice, I decided to train for the ministry in the Missouri Synod rather than escaping to a more moderate denomination.

Concordia's strength was biblical exegesis. The faculty was grounded in the Christian gospel and was helping the Missouri Synod become more open-minded. I served a year as a student pastor in Omaha, Nebraska, working mainly with low- and middle-income teenagers.

Just before I graduated from seminary, aggressive conservatives in the Missouri Synod launched a purge. They fired the seminary's president. Nearly all the faculty and three-quarters of the students eventually left our campus and formed Concordia Seminary in Exile.

The Missouri Synod was going through a schism, so most of the students graduating from the Seminary in

Exile couldn't find paying positions. The congregation I had served in Omaha couldn't support me, but they ordained me as a missionary-economist—charging me to connect Christian faith and moral teaching to economics, especially poverty issues. The Lutheran World Federation gave me a scholarship to study economics at the London School of Economics. That led to a degree and my second book, *Where Faith and Economics Meet.*

The Lutheran World Federation hired me to work for the Rangpur Dinajpur Rural Service in Bangladesh. Janet and I moved to Thakurgaon, a small town in northwest Bangladesh. I evaluated problems in a silk production project. I learned some Bengali and then spent four months in a tiny rural settlement, trying to come up with new approaches for the agency. I mainly learned how difficult it is for very poor people to take advantage of development opportunities. Their cattle are too weak to pull improved plows. If a person can't read, it's hard to think systematically about how to improve your life.

Janet is grateful for our time in Bangladesh, but living in rural Bangladesh was tougher for her than me. Women don't have much freedom, and that includes foreign women. She taught English to a group of girls at a high school near our home.

On a visit to Calcutta we met Mother Teresa. She was pleased to meet a Lutheran. "The Lutherans send me blankets," she explained. My mother was part of a quilting group at her church in Nebraska that made blankets for Lutheran World Relief, and I find it wonderful that what Mother Teresa knew about Lutherans was that they sent her blankets.

When I talk with young adults now, they sometimes express interest in my young adult years. Based on my experience, it makes sense to explore and tackle problems that seem important, even if it isn't clear how these activities will fit together into a career. These explorations will help address a pressing issue and may move the young person to the cutting edge of needed changes. My checkered set of experiences prepared me for a career I could not have planned.

A Preacher at the World Bank

While Janet and I were in Bangladesh I was offered a position at the World Bank. The World Bank is an intergovernmental institution that provides financing and advice to developing countries. It is a major center of knowledge about development, and I thought it would be a good place to spend a few years and learn about macro issues that affect poor people. I ended up serving as an economist there for fifteen years, working almost entirely on poverty reduction activities.

I worked on projects that focused on reducing urban poverty in East Africa and Latin America. I wrote speeches for Tom Clausen when he was president of the World Bank. I then played a leadership role in helping the Bank engage with nongovernmental organizations and grassroots groups around the world.

The Bank's board and management wanted the Bank to help reduce poverty, but the Bank was not always very good at it. Connecting with farmers' associations, religious groups, and organizations that advocate for the poor has now become standard practice at the Bank, but it was a fringe idea when a few colleagues and I started pushing it. The spread of democracy and the flowering of civil society in many developing countries put wind behind our sails.

At one point I was the only staffer responsible for the Bank's relationships with civil society in developing countries. The Bank now has 120 staff working in this area, and the involvement of the Bank with civil society has made it more effective in reducing poverty.

I draw two primary lessons from my experience at the World Bank. First, reform in big institutions is possible. Second, words are important. When the World Bank's president and board committed the Bank to make focused efforts to reduce poverty, the Bank didn't change in a day. But words have power. People like me were able to point to the Bank's stated purpose and work for change over many years.

I started a group of World Bank staff who met each Friday morning to discuss spiritual values and development. They came from many countries and diverse religious backgrounds. Occasionally members of the group worked together from their different positions within the Bank on reform issues. Four of us—a Hindu, a Muslim, a Christian, and a secular person—wrote a book together about this long-running interfaith dialogue, *Friday Morning Reflections at the World Bank*. The Friday morning group continued to meet for thirty years.

How Bread for the World Has Shaped Me

While I was still at the World Bank, a Bread for the World intern helped me write a book on service in developing countries. I later became a member of Bread's board.

When Arthur Simon, Bread's founder, decided to step aside from the leadership of Bread for the World, I felt that this was the job for which God made me. My initial salary at Bread for the World was about a third of what I had been earning at the World Bank, and the drop in salary intensified my sense of vocation.

I continue to love my work at Bread for three reasons. First, the effort I invest has a big impact among hungry and poor people. Second, I think we have a good chance to overcome mass hunger and poverty. I expect to see the number of hungry people in the world drop dramatically in my lifetime. Third, it's important to me that Bread for the World does this work in the name of Jesus and to the glory of God.

My years at Bread have allowed me to watch history unfold from the perspective of what's good for poor and hungry people: "What is Congress doing, and how will that affect hungry people?" I'm convinced that's a question that God asks. Poor people themselves don't usually notice what's going on in Congress. They're busy with their own lives. They may not see when Congress makes a decision that is going to make their lives much harder. Bread for the World's work gives you a God's-angle-of-vision perspective on history.

This is sometimes depressing, because Congress makes many decisions with little thought to their impact among poor people. Each member of Congress is besieged with pressures to serve various interests. It's not that anybody wants people to go hungry, but what's good for hungry kids seldom gets much attention. On Bread for the World issues, the problem is often not opposition. The problem is getting five minutes of a senator's time.

On the other hand, the Bread angle-of-vision has given me opportunities to see God at work. First of all, God sustains hungry and poor people. How can it be that year after year they are neglected by those of us who have power and money, and yet they are sustained? They pray to God to provide them with food, and the abundance of God's creation allows them to get food. The sun shines on everyone, poor and rich alike. If it were up to politicians in Washington or investors in New York, maybe the sun wouldn't shine without price. But the sun does shine on everybody, so there's fruit for Africans and beautiful weather that even homeless people can enjoy. Joy, energy, and determination well up within people. These, too, are free gifts from God.

Beyond that, God sometimes moves the hearts of people who can change things. With some frequency, powerful people say, "Yes, I'll do that." It was not in the interest of Jim Leach to introduce debt relief or of Spencer Bacchus to become a champion for debt relief. Why would they do such a thing? When Leach agreed to introduce debt relief, the first thing he said was, "I'll do this one for St. Paul. Somebody's got to do these things now that Paul Simon is not in Congress anymore." Senator Paul Simon, now deceased, was the brother of Bread for the World's founder, Arthur Simon.

So God moves people in power, and, most important, God moves us. Bread for the World's network of individuals and churches is moved to speak up for poor and hungry people, and we win a lot. I hope this book and the accompanying Web site engage many people more deeply in God's movement to end mass hunger and poverty.

My Two Sons

Janet and I are blessed with a loving family. We have two adopted sons, and they have changed how I think about lots of things, including hunger and poverty.

When my older son, Andrew, got in touch with his birth mother, she almost immediately joined Bread for the World. When we met her, we learned why. She was a graduate student when she became pregnant with Andrew. She did not have much money. She depended on the WIC program to help her maintain a nutritious diet. That was in the early

1980s. Bread for the World members had campaigned in the 1970s to launch and expand WIC, and they campaigned in the early 1980s to block cuts to this program.

Andrew is an exceptionally bright and creative young man. If WIC had not helped his birth mother, my son might not be as bright and creative as he is. So I am myself a beneficiary of Bread for the World's advocacy efforts.

Andrew is gay. He came out the month he graduated from high school. Andrew's gay rights activism has made me more aware and appreciative of the abundant diversity among people.

We always knew that Andrew's birth father was from Iran. He was a graduate student in the United States when Andrew was conceived. Andrew has developed a relationship with his birth father, now a professor in Tehran, and with his half-cousins. The family invited him to meet them in Dubai (on the Persian Gulf). Then last year Andrew and I both vacationed with them in Turkey. So I now have a family link to people on the other side of the globe.

My second son, John, is in recovery from alcoholism and addiction. Addiction is a terrible, genetic, often fatal disease. When John was in active addiction, we eventually had to distance ourselves from him. He became poor and sometimes hungry. When he ended up homeless, there was nothing I could do to help.

Thankfully he decided to get sober and go back to a halfway house. Through Alcoholics Anonymous, John has had a spiritual awakening. He has to make his own way in the world and isn't yet earning much money. But he is a new man—more obviously "born again" than anyone I've ever known. He prays on his knees morning and night, and he is active in helping other people who are recovering from addiction. I am immensely proud of John and grateful to God for guiding his steps.

John's experience has given me an up-close view of some

of the harsh aspects of poverty—boarding houses with bed bugs, for example, and employers who won't let low-wage workers work full-time. Now that John is rebuilding his life, I feel even more urgently the importance of a full-employment economy and programs that give struggling people a chance to move forward with their lives.

John's addiction has made me more aware of mental and physical disabilities and their role in making many people poor. Physical disabilities are obvious, but mental health problems also contribute to employment and family problems that lead to poverty and, in some cases, to homelessness and prison. Our family was able to pay for drug treatment, but many families cannot, and affordable mental health services would help. I have become a big supporter of drug courts, which provide both therapy and strict discipline for alcoholics and addicts.

As the father of an addict, I have also learned that people make their own choices and that nobody can do much to help someone who is caught up in self-destructive behavior. The addiction of a family member drives other members of the family crazy—or, alternatively, to a deeper reliance on God.

Alcoholics, addicts, and their family members learn that our lives are out of control, and the twelve steps of Alcoholics Anonymous encourage us to ask our Higher Power—whether we talk about God or have a different understanding—to help. We examine ourselves morally, and ask the Higher Power to remove our faults. We make amends to people we have hurt, and commit ourselves to service—living one day at a time, always asking our Higher Power for guidance.

John's fierce reliance on God has influenced me to be less confident about my own efforts and more fervent in prayer that God will help my family and all other people in their needs.

My Next Step

I am this year being awarded the World Food Prize in recognition of what Bread for the World's members and churches have achieved for hungry people. I am sharing this year's prize with Jo Luck, who has led a major expansion of what Heifer International does to develop agriculture among poor people worldwide.

The publication of this book is the next step in my life and work. At this moment of exceptional need and opportunity I plan to travel around the country and use mass media to help stir up grassroots activism to change the politics of hunger and poverty.

CHAPTER 10

TAKE A STEP

God is on His knees to us, waiting for us to turn around this super-tanker of indifference, our own indifference a lot of the time.

Bono

You wouldn't be reading this book if you weren't already committed. Like me, you have been drawn into the movement to overcome hunger and poverty, and you understand the importance of political change. I am praying that you will help to stir up a stronger political constituency for hungry and poor people, and that we will together bend history toward justice over the next few years.

This chapter discusses lots of ways that you can deepen your involvement and increase your impact. Political activism needs to be grounded in spirituality, service, and self-education, so this chapter offers a broad menu of ways we can deepen our engagement. It closes with specific suggestions about various ways you can change the politics of hunger now.

You may well feel that you are already overcommitted, but you can still consider shifting time and energy to higher-impact activities. And truth be told, nearly all of us could be more generous with our time and energy than we are.

Ground Yourself in God

We're not going to change the world unless we get our prayers right. Whenever you pray, "Give us this day our daily bread," include hungry people in our country and around the world in your petition. Pray that God will come into your life in a new way and use you for God's purposes in the world. When you take communion, remember that the body of Christ is broken for all people—and that this meal is a mandate to make sure that everybody has enough to eat.

Anybody who is trying to maintain faith and commitment needs devotional times alone. By nature I'm more inclined to action than prayer, but leading Bread for the World—and my personal struggles—have driven me to a daily time of prayer and to lots of mini-prayers as my days unfold.

Yet I still find my best inspiration in going to church every Sunday morning. Sitting together with Janet in a congregation of believers I listen to Bible readings and a sermon about them. We pray for our own needs and the needs of the world. We share in the bread and wine that sustain our souls. We talk with friends about our lives, what is going on in the world, and the ministries of the congregation.

Most people need other people to help them connect to God. Religious Americans are three to four times more likely to be involved in the community than nonreligious Americans. They are more apt to work on community projects, attend public meetings, vote in local elections, go to political rallies, and donate to causes. But social scientists find that these civic behaviors depend less on the specifics of what we believe than on the fact that we are part of a religious congregation and make friends there. Friends at church pray for us, encourage us, and ask us to do things for the community.[1]

Lots of people say they are spiritual but not religious. But we need a religious congregation or some other moral community to help us be truly spiritual.

You can be a leader on social issues within your congregation. You can promote the social ministries of your church. You can organize Christian education programs or help plan worship services. Hungry and poor people are close to the heart of God, so they should be prominent in the prayers, hymns, and sermons of every church. You can help your church make itself a welcoming place for diverse people, including low-income people.

Your church body and related organizations almost certainly offer materials and programs to encourage you and your congregation to help hungry and poor people. If you are part of the Evangelical Lutheran Church of America, for example, check out your denomination's hunger program, its Washington office, Lutheran Services in America, and Lutheran World Relief. If you are part of the Presbyterian Church (U.S.A.), you too have a strong hunger program, and Presbyterian Women is a great resource. If you are Catholic, you can draw great resources from the U.S. Conference of Catholic Bishops, Catholic Charities, Catholic Relief Services, the Catholic Health Association, and NETWORK. There's a strong trend in U.S. religion toward independent congregations, but resources from national church bodies and agencies will help people in your church think bigger than their own lives and community.

Help, with an Eye toward Change

Our work for social change should include direct assistance to people in need. How can we be committed to overcoming hunger and poverty without being involved with hungry and poor individuals? Our efforts for social change will be better motivated and informed if they are grounded in experience with particular individuals and communities.

For starters we need to take care of ourselves and those close to us. Nearly all of us go through times in our lives when we need to focus on our own needs or the needs of family members. There is also need all around us. An elderly woman in my neighborhood needs a little help to keep her life going and is short of cash.

You can also get involved in one of your church's community ministries or support a community agency. Look especially for community programs that help needy people become self-reliant (such as teaching English to immigrants) or that empower poor people (a local housing coalition, for example).

Community agencies such as Catholic Charities and the Salvation Army provide desperately needed help on a large scale. It's also important to support international charities such as Church World Service, Catholic Relief Services, or the International Rescue Committee.

The traditional tithe—giving 10 percent of your income to church and charities—is a helpful standard. On average, church members in the United States give away only 2.58 percent of their income.[2] If church members would double their current giving to 5 percent, that would amount to about $60 billion more each year. That in itself would go a long way toward overcoming hunger and poverty.

Arthur Simon, the founder of Bread for the World, often says that action against hunger walks on two legs: assistance and advocacy. So if you tutor a low-income child once a week, write a letter to your member of Congress about some hunger or poverty issue every other week. If you write a check to an international charity, write a letter to Congress about a global poverty issue that same day.

People often ask me what charities I consider most effective. In my experience, most established charities use the donations they receive effectively. Bread for the World gets high marks from charity evaluation Web sites (such as Charity Navigator), and they can help you check for problems at a charity you don't know well. But the best way to assess a charity is to become familiar with it. Over time you learn from a charity you support about how they work and what they achieve. Effective donors give to a limited number of organizations and stick with them over time. You can also check out the list of board members. Are they people you trust? The board members of charities related to church bodies will be church leaders, and any church body must maintain the trust of its people.

I favor charities that are involved in advocacy and that empower poor people to influence policies that affect them. I recommend that every charitable organization spend 5 percent of its budget to educate its supporters about the problems it is addressing and another 5 percent to influence government policies that affect the people it serves. If every charity would give a tithe of its budget to education and advocacy, they would create the U.S. public and political will that is needed to make dramatic progress against hunger and poverty in our country and around the world. Ask the charities you support what they are doing to speak up for the people they serve.

Shape Your Life
to Your Values

Our pattern of living should reflect our values. We can live economically, in order to free up time and money to help people in need.

We can also be careful about our impact on the environment. Much of the rest of the world is copying aspects of the typical U.S. lifestyle, and the earth cannot bear the impact of billions more people doing as much environmental damage as we do. When millions of individuals and families make modest changes, it has a significant macro impact. It also raises awareness and increases support for changes in public policies that will have an even bigger impact on the environment.

We can be thoughtful about what we eat. Most Americans are struggling to lose weight, and we nearly all fall short of our goals. This suggests that society will eventually have to make structural changes to complement individual motivation. These could range from more emphasis on physical education in schools to a broad reorganization of how we live and work so that people get more exercise in their daily routine. In the meantime, the evidence is clear about what we ought to do: make a lasting shift to fewer calories and more exercise.

Feeling guilty and temporary diets don't help. Motivational support from a group program such as Weight Watchers can help. Prayer can also help. Saying a prayer of thanks every time we eat may help us enjoy food in a healthy way—and remember that some people don't have enough to eat.

Many of us are buying more locally grown foods and raising some of our own vegetables. Some people are opting for organic foods or a vegetarian diet. The main motivations are usually freshness and health. But a change in diet can also be a meaningful protest against ethical issues in the U.S. food system. If we eat locally grown food, we reduce the environmental cost of transporting tomatoes from far away. If we eat lower on the food chain—grain instead of meat—we also reduce our environmental footprint. It takes six thousand calories of grain feed to produce one thousand calories of meat.[3]

50 Ways to Help Save the Earth: How You and Your Church Can Make a Difference (Westminster John Knox Press, 2009) provides a shower of ideas about lifestyle and other ways to contribute to social change. It's an easy read—and hard to put down. I also recommend *Our Day to End Poverty: 24 Ways You Can Make a Difference*, by Shannon Daley-Harris and Jeffery Keenan (Berrett-Koehler Publishers, 2007).

Learn for a Better World

We need to keep learning about the problems poor people confront and strategies to solve them, so continue reading about these issues and pay attention to the news.

Those of us who have plenty often get caught up in our own lives and in the lives of friends who also have plenty. Concentrations of poverty tend to be hidden away in regions or parts of our cities that better-off people seldom visit. We're even farther away from the severe poverty of developing countries. So how can we learn about hunger and poverty in a close-up, personal way?

One way is regular, prayerful volunteer work. Jeffry Korgen, a director of social ministries in a Catholic diocese, asked his colleagues across the country what really works to engage Catholics in social justice.[4] Their collective experience is that personal engagement with people in need is critical, and that religious devotion must be part of the experience. Jesus said that when we help hungry people, we are helping him (Matthew 25), and religious devotion allows believers to recognize Jesus in poor people with whom they are working. If we don't actually spend time with poor people, we can't meet Jesus in them. And if we don't take care to maintain a spiritual perspective, we may also fail to see Jesus. Some people volunteer briefly, but give up with a hardened view that poor people are mainly to blame for their own problems.

In this era of international travel and communication we can also become personally engaged with poor people in other countries. More than 5 million Americans are living abroad, and 63 million travel abroad in a typical year.[5]

Rick Steves, the host of *Europe through the Back Door* on public television, is an active member of Bread for the World. Rick urges Americans to travel in a way that allows them to meet local people. He teaches a style of travel that expands the traveler's mind. Since the terrorist attacks of 2001, Rick has put increasing emphasis on the most important lessons of travel. Traveling teaches Americans that people in other countries have different, sometimes better ways to do things. It teaches us to think globally, making us more aware of the needs of poor people around the world. He writes about these ideas in his book *Travel as a Political Act.*[6]

A growing number of Americans find ways to spend time with poor people and programs that help them. My son Andrew has gone to Malawi twice to work as a volunteer with World Camp. He has helped conduct AIDS education programs, mainly in high schools, and this has been life-changing for him. His experience included living with Malawian families. He knew that only 2 percent of Malawi households have electricity, but he learned that in a different way when the sun went down and it got *very* dark in the village. Like most other Americans who spend time with poor people in a developing country, Andrew was inspired by the joy and generosity of many of the people he met.

Many Christian congregations and programs now organize short-term mission trips, and 1.6 million churchgoers go each year on mission trips to Asia, Africa, or Latin America.[7] The Americans may paint a building or do some other task for a local church or agency. Prayer and religious devotion are part of the experience. People make friends locally, and they can stay in touch with them via the Web when they return home.

People-to-people relationships like this are deeply satisfying, especially for the Americans involved. The Americans and their local hosts learn from each other. The Americans become familiar with a program and then support it financially when they get home. They may invite their overseas counterparts to visit them in the United States. On the other hand, most of the money spent on a short-term mission trip covers the cost of travel, and Americans visiting a country for the first time aren't likely to help that much.

Bread for the World offers a resource—*Getting Ready to Come Back*—to help people in short-term mission programs reflect on the economic and political aspects of development and on how we can use our influence with the U.S. government to help friends in poor countries. It encourages mission groups to learn about the country they will visit and how our country's policies and programs affect it. When they return home they can meet with their members of Congress to share what they learned. Participants in short-term mission programs also can become members of Bread for the World, so that their ongoing partnership with the people they visit includes advocacy on poverty issues.

Make It Your Job

You might be able to make a difference for hungry and poor people at your place of work. If you are a teacher, for example, you may be able to educate your students on hunger and poverty issues.

If you are in business, can you urge your company to provide adequate salary and benefits to all employees? Is there a way your business can help hungry and poor people through its operations—by extending its services to struggling families, for example? Is there a feasible, perhaps even profitable change in operations that would increase your company's impact among people in need— perhaps opening a facility in a low-income neighborhood? Could your company's president communicate with your members of Congress about a poverty-related issue?

We aren't going to end mass hunger and poverty until some for-profit companies identify with the cause and feature hunger in their advertising and philanthropy, as some companies now feature the environment. We also need some businesspeople and companies to be advocates with Congress on behalf of hungry and poor people. Some businesses stand to prosper as the United States or developing countries reduce poverty, but even these businesses seldom help advocacy groups with Congress.

Over time you might be able to shape your career toward work that is focused on people in need. The personal satisfaction you gain may make it worth settling for less income.

Change the Politics of Hunger

The rest of this chapter suggests ways you can directly change the politics of hunger. I especially hope that you will take me up on suggestions from these final sections. It's also important that you consider ways to ground political work and advocacy in the overall pattern of your life. But we have a chance to change our nation's politics and policies on hunger and poverty issues right now, so we need a surge in activism now.

The main way our country decides on national priorities is through elections. Some people imagine that elections don't matter much or that all politicians are the same. But who gets elected definitely makes a big difference. Which party controls the House or Senate makes a huge difference.

Voting is a sacred obligation. Giving time and money to candidates who have demonstrated their commitment to reducing mass hunger and poverty is an integral part of good stewardship. Very few Americans are active in political parties. But the political parties pull the nation in different directions, and people who are active in one of the parties have a disproportionate impact on the future.

When you contribute time or money to a campaign, you will also have the ear of the candidate if she is elected. I've watched Terry Meehan, a Bread for the World board member who makes substantial contributions to candidates, use his access to politicians to advance hunger issues. It works. The husband of a former board member volunteered most of his time for a whole year to help a candidate get elected to the Senate for the first time. Many years later, he can call that senator at his home to talk about Bread for the World issues.

The two major parties are now evenly matched. Power shifts back and forth with each election. This has made elections even more important than they were in periods when one party was dominant.

You can also change the politics of hunger through advocacy organizations. At the national level, Bread for the World is one of a growing number of advocacy organizations that tackle hunger and poverty issues. Other organizations that help grassroots people get engaged include the ONE Campaign (www.one.org), RESULTS (www.results.org), and NETWORK (www.networklobby.org). Your church body or a charity you support may maintain an advocacy network. Some of the best advocates get information from more than one organization.

All of these advocacy groups work in a bipartisan way, encouraging Republicans and Democrats to work together for hungry people. At a time of sharp division between the two parties, bipartisan advocacy has become more difficult and more important.

Hunger and poverty are related to many other issues: children, the environment, peace, campaign finance reform, and more. Various advocacy organizations focus on each of these issues. None of us can do everything, so pick one or two areas of concern that especially move you and work in those areas over a period of years.

Advocacy for poor people at state legislatures is usually weaker than advocacy at the federal level, so you might join an advocacy network that focuses on your state legislature. States and local governments cannot run up a deficit like the federal government can, so they slash budgets in hard times. Especially at those times, advocates need to be in touch with their state legislators about programs that are important to poor and vulnerable people.

Industrial Areas Foundation (www.industrialareas foundation.org) and PICO (www.piconetwork.org) have helped build many community organizations over the last two decades. Local religious congregations are typically the building blocks. These organizations help low- and middle-income communities agree on priorities and speak up for themselves. The focus is usually on local issues, but some of these organizations are increasingly engaged in state and national issues, too. These community organizations and their increasing involvement in national issues have been an important change for the better in the politics of U.S. poverty.

In some states or communities, there are coalitions that focus specifically on hunger or food security. When the many agencies in a community that feed hungry people think together about long-term solutions, they often see ways to shift some of their effort to have a bigger impact. They almost always strengthen their capacity for advocacy.

If you want to know about organizations that address poverty and hunger issues in your community or state, call your local council of churches, interfaith council, or Catholic diocesan office. You can also ask the Bread for the World organizers for your region.

Efforts to change the politics of hunger require both people and money. As I have studied the history of anti-hunger advocacy, I have been struck by how often promising organizations went out of business because of money trouble. Political campaigns also cost money; if and when our country manages to reduce the role of money in elections, candidates for election will still need financial support. Most of us could get more impact with our charitable donations by shifting more of our dollars to social change and political purposes.

Bread for the World

Joining in the work of Bread for the World is one of the best ways to drive change on hunger and poverty issues. Here's our contact information:

Bread for the World
425 3rd Street SW
Washington, DC 20001
1-800-82BREAD
www.bread.org

Become Part of Bread for the World

We need you, especially now. If you become a member, you'll receive Bread's newsletter in the mail or on-line. You can also become part of Bread's online community and social networking activities or listen to Bread's monthly podcast. We provide brief, balanced information on current hunger issues. We also alert you when a letter or phone call to your particular member of Congress will have the biggest impact, and we keep you informed about new resources for hunger education and advocacy — such as Bread for the World Institute's annual hunger report.

Writing a letter to Congress is easy to do, and letters to Congress make a real difference. Look back to page 109 for information on how to communicate effectively with your members of Congress.

Engage Your Church

You can help your church or campus group get engaged in advocacy for hungry people. Bread's Web site has great resources for awareness building and education in churches. Every year Bread for the World takes up an Offering of Letters in churches across the country. This has proved to be an effective way to mobilize lots of letters to Congress and drive change. It will also add a needed dimension to the life of your church. Bread provides a kit that will give you everything you need to mobilize letter writing in your church.

Become a Bread Activist

Bread for the World's network includes active volunteers in every congressional district in the country. We look to them for leadership—to enlist local congregations, get coverage and support from local media, and meet face-to-face with their members of Congress. We are especially eager to recruit more young people and people of color as Bread for the World leaders. In many communities, a Bread for the World group meets periodically to plan and take action together. I've been part of the local group in Northern Virginia, and I've seen firsthand how much impact a local leadership group makes.

Bread for the World's organizers are eager to support you in your advocacy and leadership within your church, campus, or community. Call 1-800-82BREAD and ask to be connected to the organizer nearest you. Our regional organizers are also listed at www.bread.org.

Contribute to Bread for the World

Money is fuel for Bread's work for hungry people. We typically win one hundred dollars in government funding for effective programs for hungry and poor people with each dollar people give to Bread. When we work for policy changes rather than funding, the impact is often even more far-reaching.

Bread for the World lobbies Congress for hungry people, so gifts to Bread for the World are not tax-deductible — but they have great impact. You can make a tax-deductible gift to Bread for the World Institute; the Institute does research and education that complements the work of Bread for the World.

One Step

This chapter has discussed lots of ways you can help, but I'd encourage you to start by deciding on one new thing that you will do for hungry and poor people. Before you set this book aside, say a prayer and decide on one step you will take, starting now.

We have set up an interactive Web site, called www .exodusfromhunger.org. You might want to go to the "My Step" page and explain the step you plan to take. That will help you live up to your commitment and inspire others.

Dick Hoehn, a former director of Bread for the World Institute, conducted in-depth interviews with outstanding Christian leaders of grassroots social justice work to find out how they became such effective advocates for poor people. In each case their stories unfolded through a series of small steps. They took an action, it had an impact, and that encouraged them to take another step.[8] They became world-changing Christians step-by-step.

Step-by-step, our lives become part of God's movement to end hunger and poverty.

CHAPTER 11

WE NEED GOD

Frankly, this chapter was an afterthought. I was getting ready to send the final manuscript to the publisher. I had checked my facts. I had refined my thinking about strategy. I had worked on making the book readable.

It's so easy for me to think that my effort, combined with my readers' response, may be enough to trigger processes that will end mass hunger in the world. Even what I had written about grounding ourselves in God focused mainly on what we can do to strengthen our faith life.

But clearly we need God to bring us into a relationship with God, and we won't overcome hunger unless this really is a movement of God in the world. We need to pray, on our knees, for God's loving presence among us, especially among people in great need.

For several decades, the world has been making dramatic progress against poverty. God has already been answering our prayers. Year after year, heroes like Connie Wick, Pat Pelham, Joe Martingale, Gyude Moore, and

Tessa Pulaski have won important, often unlikely changes in Congress. In recent years, we have received powerful help from Bono, Bill Gates, and their friends and other new allies. The economic crisis of the last few years has been a great tragedy, but it has helped to create a political environment in which we just may be able to achieve changes that will accelerate progress against hunger and poverty in our own country and around the world.

We need more surprises. Our own efforts will not, by themselves, achieve the wonderful liberation that is possible. Pray for change for hungry people, and thank God for the opportunity to be part of this great liberation.

God offers us much more than progress against hunger and poverty. God offers us divine love and purpose. God comes to people in various ways, but Jesus is my connection to God. So when it occurred to me to add this chapter to the book, I looked again at the gospel stories of Jesus feeding the hungry crowds.

The gospel writers see Jesus as a new Moses and Jesus' death and resurrection as a new exodus. Just as Moses fed the people of Israel manna in the wilderness, Jesus feeds the hungry crowd in the wilderness. Just as the people of Israel followed Moses out of slavery, now the whole world can find in Jesus our liberation from sin, death, and the forces of evil.

When Jesus miraculously fed thousands of people, the crowd got really excited. They followed Jesus eagerly. They wouldn't let him out of their sight, and they wanted to make him king. If he could provide food to everybody, this was the kind of government they wanted. But Jesus told them, "Do not work for the food that perishes, but for the food that endures for eternal life. . . . I am the bread of life" (John 6:27–35).

The core message of Christianity is that Jesus' forgiving death also counts for us—that God loves us—and that the risen Jesus will live in us. Whether we go to church regularly or are on the fringes of organized religion, opening our heart toward Jesus will give us a stronger experience of God's love than we have known before. Allowing the risen Jesus to live in us, more than we have until now, will also make us more hopeful, loving people.

One of the side benefits of Christ-in-us will be energy to change the politics of hunger and poverty.

> Almighty God, we pray for all the people who do not have enough to eat. We ask you to rescue them. Come quickly, and use us. We pray in the powerful name of Jesus. Amen

NOTES

Introduction

1. Shaohua Chen and Martin Ravallion, "The Developing World Is Poorer Than We Thought, But No Less Successful in the Fight against Poverty" (policy working paper, The World Bank, 2008). Also, conversation with Martin Ravallion, April 27, 2010.

2. Food and Agriculture Organization of the United Nations, "Prevalence of Undernourishment in Total Population" and "Number of Undernourished Persons," http://www.fao.org/economic/ess/food-security-statistics/en/. The 1970 and 2009 undernutrition data are also from the Food and Agriculture Organization of the United Nations. The 1970 and 2009 population estimates are from the U.N. Bureau of Population.

3. United Nations Children's Fund, *The State of the World's Children 2008: Child Survival*, http://www.unicef.org/publications/files/The_State_of_the_Worlds_Children_2008.pdf.

4. U.S. Census Bureau Current Population Survey, Annual Social and Economic Supplements, "Poverty Status, by Family Relationship, Race, and Hispanic Origin," http://www.census.gov/hhes/www/poverty/data/historical/people.html.

5. The Pew Research Center for the People & the Press, "The People and Their Government" (April 18, 2010), http://people-press.org/report/606/trust-in-government.

6. Estimates by Sophie Milam, a Bread for the World analyst, based on data from Feeding America and the U.S. Department of Agriculture.

7. Organization of Economic Cooperation and Development, http://webnet.oecd.org/oda2009/.

8. U.S. Conference of Catholic Bishops, *A Place at the Table: A Catholic Recommitment to Overcome Poverty and to Respect the Dignity of All God's Children* (2002), http://www.usccb.org/bishops/table.shtml.

Chapter 1: Widespread and Increased Hunger

1. United Nations Children's Fund, *Progress for Children*, 2007, http://www.unicef.org/publications/files/Progress_for_Children_No_6_revised.pdf.

2. World Bank, *World Development Indicators*, http://data.worldbank.org.

3. Deepa Narayan, et al., *Crying Out for Change: Voices of the Poor* (Oxford: Oxford University Press for the World Bank, 2000).

4. Deepa Narayan, *Moving Out of Poverty* (New York: Palgrave Macmillan, 2009).

5. U.S. Department of Agriculture, Economic Research Service, "Household Food Security in the United States, 2008," Table 1A, 2009, http://www.ers.usda.gov/Publications/ERR83/ERR83b.pdf.

6. Bread for the World Institute, "Obesity and Hunger," http://www.bread.org/learn/us-hunger-issues/obesity-and-hunger.html.

7. Christine M. Olson, "Nutrition and Health Outcomes Associated with Food Insecurity and Hunger," 1998 ASNA Symposium Proceedings, *Journal of Nutrition* 129 (1999): 521S–524S.

8. U.S. Department of Agriculture, Economic Research Service, "Household Food Security in the United States, 2008," Table 1B, 2009, http://www.ers.usda.gov/Publications/ERR83/ERR83b.pdf.

9. J. Larry Brown, Donald Shepard, Timothy Martin, John Orwat, *The Economic Cost of Domestic Hunger*, Sodexho Foundation, 2007, http://www.sodexofoundation.org/hunger_us/Images/Cost%20of%20Domestic%20Hunger%20Report%20_tcm150-155150.pdf.

10. U.S. Department of Agriculture, Economic Research Service, "Household Food Security in the United States, 2008," Table 1B.

11. Isabell Sawhill and Ron Haskins, "5 Myths about Our Land of Opportunity," *Washington Post*, November 1, 2009, B5.

12. Ron Sider, *Just Generosity* (Grand Rapids: Baker Books, 1999), 125–26.

13. Mark Greenberg, "Making Poverty History," *Ending Poverty in America*, American Prospect Special Report, 2007, 4, http://www.prospect.org/cs/articles?article=making_poverty_history.

14. Stephen Pimpare, *A People's History of Poverty in America* (New York: New Books, 2008), 113, 232.

15. U.N. Food and Agriculture Organization, "How to Feed the World in 2050," 2009, http://www.fao.org/fileadmin/templates/wsfs/docs/expert_paper/How_to_Feed_the_World_in_2050.pdf.

16. Bread for the World Institute, *Hunger Report 2008: Working Harder for Working Families* (Washington, DC: Bread for the World, 2008), 79–87.

17. Ronald Reagan, "To Restore America," speech delivered March 31, 1976, http://www.pbs.org/wgbh/amex/reagan/sfeature/quotes.html.

18. The Alliance to End Hunger, "Voters say, 'Put the needs of Americans first,'" http://www.alliancetoendhunger.org/TheAlliancetoEndHunger_jan-2010-poll.htm.

Chapter 2: Dramatic Progress Is Feasible

1. J. Vandemoortele, "The MDGs," *WIDER Angle* (2007): 6–7, http://www.thefreelibrary.com/The+MDGs:+%27M%27+for+misunderstood%3F-a0163836883. Also, personal communication with Brian Atwood, who was administrator of USAID as the Millennium Development Goals were taking shape.

2. Lake Snell Perry & Associates, "Developing Messages about Humanitarian and Development Assistance," April 2004, InterAction, Global Health Council, Bread for the World, and BetterSaferWorld, www.globalhealth.org/docs/summary_presentation.ppt.

3. Organization for Economic Cooperation and Development, Development Assistance Committee, http://stats.oecd.org/wbos/Index.aspx?DatasetCode=ODA_DONOR. See also United Nations, *The Millennium Development Goals Report 2009* (New York: United Nations 2009), 48–49, http://www.un.org/millenniumgoals/pdf/MDG_Report_2009_ENG.pdf.

4. Organization for Economic Cooperation and Development, *The Paris Declaration on Aid Effectiveness*, 2005, http://www.oecd.org/dataoecd/11/41/34428351.pdf.

5. U.N. Millennium Project, *Investing in Development: A Practical Plan to Achieve the Millennium Development Goals* (2005), http://www .unmillenniumproject.org/documents/overviewEngLowRes.pdf.

6. United Nations, *The Millennium Development Goals Report 2008* and *Addendum* (New York: United Nations, 2008).

7. Branko Milanovic, *Global Income Inequality* (Washington, DC: World Bank, 2006), 14–16.

8. Washington, DC: Center for Global Development (forthcoming).

9. World Health Organization, *Scaling Up Priority HIV/AIDS Interventions in the Health Sector*, 2008, http://www.who.int/hiv/ mediacentre/2008progressreport/en/index.html.

10. Freedom House, *Freedom in the World 2002*, http://freedomhouse .org/template.cfm?page=130&year=2002; *Freedom in the World 2008*, http://www.freedomhouse.org/template.cfm?page=130&year=2008.

11. Human Security Centre, *Human Security Report 2005* (New York: Oxford University Press, 2005), iii.

12. Sandeep Mahajan, *Bangladesh: Strategy for Sustained Growth* (Washington: World Bank, 2007), http://go.worldbank.org/ 64BPMVS7B0 .

13. Stephen Pimpare, *A People's History of Poverty in America* (New York: New Books, 2008), 235.

14. Paul Krugman, "The Great Wealth Transfer," *Rolling Stone*, November 30, 2006, http://www.rollingstone.com/politics/story ./12699486/paul_krugman_on_the_great_wealth_transfer_5great_ wealth_transfer.

15. Michael B. Katz, *The Undeserving Poor: From the War on Poverty to the War on Welfare* (New York: Pantheon Books, 1989), 187.

16. Nick Kotz, *Hunger in America* (New York: Field Foundation, 1979), cited by Dorothy Rosenbaum and Zoe Neuberger, "Food and Nutrition Programs," Center on Budget and Policy Priorities, 2005, http://www.cbpp.or/7-19-05fa.htm.

17. Katz, *Undeserving Poor*, 113.

18. Bread for the World Institute, *Hunger Report 2008: Working Harder for Working Families* (Washington, DC: Bread for the World, 2008), 16–38.

19. Elizabeth Arias, Brian Rostron, and Betzaida Tejada-Vera, "United States Life Tables," *National Vital Statistics Reports* 54, no. 10

(Centers for Disease Control and Prevention, 2010), 34, http://www
.cdg.gov/nchs/data/nvsr/nvsr58/nvsr58_10.pdf. Also, U.S. Census
Bureau, "Current Population Survey, Annual Social and Economic
Supplements," Table A-2, http://www.census.gov/population/
socdemo/education/cps2008/tabA-2.xls.

20. World Bank, *World Development Indicators*, http://www.data
.worldbank.org., http://ddp-ext.worldbank.org/ext/DDPQQ/report
.do?method=showReport.

21. Center on Budget and Policy Priorities, "Where Do Our Federal Tax Dollars Go?" 2009, http://www.cbpp.org/cms/index
.cfm?fa+view&id=1258.

22. American Pet Products Association, "Industry Statistics
and Trends," http://www.americanpetproducts.org/press_
industrytrends.asp.

23. Nobel Peace Prize Lecture. December 11, 1964, http://
nobelprize.org/nobel_prizes/peace/laureates/1964/king-lecture.html.

Chapter 3: Countries That Have Reduced Hunger and Poverty

1. Jeffrey Sachs, *The End of Poverty* (New York: Penguin Press,
2005), 26–50.

2. L. S. Stavrianos, *Global Rift* (New York: Morrow, 1981).

3. Eric Munoz, Salik Farooqi, Dulce Gamboa, and Emily
Nohner from Bread for the World Institute's staff helped develop
these country studies.

4. World Bank, *World Development Indicators*, http://data
.worldbank.org.

5. Martin Ravallin, "Are There Lessons for Africa from
China's Success Against Poverty?" 2008, http://www.oecd.org/
dataoecd/27/8/40378144.pdf.

6. U.N. Statistics Division, "U.N. Millennium Development Goals
Indicators," http://mdgs.un.org/unsd/mdg/SeriesDetail
.aspx?srid=589&crid=156.

7. Carin Zissis and Jayshree Bajoria, "China's Environmental
Crisis," Council on Foreign Relations, 2007, http://www.cfr.org/
publication/12608/chinas_environmental_crisis.html#1.

8. Ma Yan, *The Diary of Ma Yan* (New York: Harper Collins, 2005).

9. W. Nubin, ed., *Sri Lanka: Current Issues and Historical Background* (New York: Nova Science Publishers, 2003), 29.

10. World Heath Organization, "The Safe Motherhood Initiative Reduces Maternal Deaths in Sri Lanka," *Health: A Key to Prosperity—Success Stories in Developing Countries*, http://www.who.int/inf-new/mate1.htm.

11. World Bank, *World Development Indicators*.

12. United Nations Development Programme, "Mozambique: National Human Development Report 2005, 2006, http://hdr.undp.org/rss/reports/nationalreports/africa/mozambique/MOZAMBIQUE_2005_en.pdf.

13. World Bank, *World Development Indicators*.

14. Fabio Veras Soares, Rafael Perez Ribas, and Rafael Guerreiro Osorio, "Evaluating the Impact of Brazil's *Bolsa Família*," 2007, http://www.undp-povertycentre.org/pub/IPCEvaluationNote1.pdf. Also, Anthony Hall, "From Fome Zero to Bolsa Família," *Journal of Latin American Studies* 38, no. 4 (November 2006): 689.

15. David Beckmann and Emily Byers, *Building Political Will to End Hunger*, Prepared for the U.N. Millennium Project Hunger Task Force (Washington, DC: Bread for the World Institute, 2004).

16. S. G. Rappaport, "Change and Continuity in Attention to Poverty in Mexico" in *Changing Structure of Mexico*, ed. Laura Randall (Armonk, NY: M. E. Sharpe, 2006).

17. Santiago Levy, *Progress against Poverty: Sustaining Mexico's Progresa-Oportunidades* (Washington, DC: Brookings Institution Press, 2006), 33–80.

18. World Bank, *World Development Indicators*.

19. Bread for the World Institute, *Hunger Report 2009: Global Development—Charting a New Course* (Washington, DC: Bread for the World, 2008), 76.

20. Todd Post, "Setting a Goal to End Poverty and Hunger in the United States," Bread for the World Institute, 2009, 6.

21. Cathy Newman, "June Budget 2010: Housing Benefit, Child Poverty, and Taxes," http://blogs.channel4.com/factcheck/2010/06/22/the-budget-factchecked-housing-benefit-child-poverty-and-taxes/.

22. Kathleen Beegle, "The Real Costs of Indonesia's Economic Crisis," 2008, siteresources.worldbank.org/ INTECAREGTOPMACGRO/Resources/KathleenBeegle.ppt. See also Embassy of the United States in Indonesia, "Chronology of the Crisis," http://jakarta.usembassy.gov/econ/crisis.html.

Chapter 4: This Is God Moving in Our Time

1. New York: HarperCollins, 1994.

2. Martin Luther King, III, "Realizing the Dream in the Middle East," speech at Peres Center for Peace, Jaffa, Israel, April 2010, quoted in The King Center for Nonviolent Social Change, *Global Nonviolence Initiative: Israel and Palestine, April 2010*, http://www .realizingthedream.org/where-we-work/project-reports/Israel-Palestine%20External%20Report-April%202010.pdf/view.

3. I asked a diverse group of Christian theologians—Jose Irizarry, Vincent Miller, Earl Trent, Cheri Holdridge, Gary Cook, and Christine Pohl—to reflect on the claim that God is moving in history to overcome hunger and poverty. They raised questions and helped me think more clearly, but they all found this message consistent with their own thinking about God.

4. James L. McDonald, "Hope in a Time of Calamity," sermon at Garden Memorial Presbyterian Church, July 27, 2008.

5. Taylor Branch, *Parting the Waters* (New York: Simon & Schuster), 162.

Chapter 5: Getting Serious about Poverty Would Be Good for America

1. See, for example, Bruce Gilley, *The Right to Rule: How States Win and Lose Legitimacy* (New York: Columbia University Press, 2009).

2. Duncan Green, *From Poverty to Power* (Oxford: Oxfam, 2008), 96.

3. Bread for the World Institute, *Hunger Report 2009: Global Development—Charting a New Course* (Washington, DC: Bread for the World, 2009), 118–20.

4. Center for Global Development, *Commitment to Development Index 2008*, http://www.cgdev.org/section/initiatives/_active/cdi/_non_flash/.

5. Quoted in Robert N. Bellah, "Individualism and Commitment in American Life," February 20, 1986, http://robertbellah.com/lectures_4.htm.

6. Herbert Hoover, "Rugged Individualism," speech delivered October 22, 1928, http://www.pinzler.com/ushistory/ruggedsupp.html.

7. Bill Gates, speech at George Washington University, December 3, 2008, http://www.gatesfoundation.org/speeches-commentary/Pages/bill-gates-2008-george-washington-university-speech.aspx.

8. Salik Farooqi, a Bread for the World Institute analyst, combined data on the Islamic Conference countries with estimates for India and China to arrive at this figure.

9. Susan Rice, "The Threat of Global Poverty," *National Journal* (Spring 2006): 76.

10. Robert J. Samuelson, "The Rich and the Rest," *Washington Post*, April 19, 2007; Harold Meyerson, "Rise of the Have-Nots," *Washington Post*, September 26, 2007; and Bread for the World Institute, *Hunger Report 2008: Working Harder for Working Families* (Washington, DC: Bread for the World, 2008), 3.

Chapter 6: People of Faith Can Make Congress Work

1. "Commencement Address to the Class of 2009," University of Portland, May 21, 2009, http://www.up.edu/commencement/default.aspx?cid=9456&pid=3144.

2. Barbara Devaney, Linda Bilheimer, and Jennifer Schore, "The Savings in Medicaid Costs for Newborns and Their Mothers Resulting from Prenatal Participation in the WIC Program," Food and Nutrition Service of the U.S. Department of Agriculture, October 1991, http://www.fns.usda.gov/ora/MENU/Published/WIC/FILES/savadd.pdf.

3. U.S. Agency for International Development, "Child Health: Saving Lives, Protecting Health," http://www.usaid.gov/our_work/global_health/mch/ch/index.html Also, "Two Decades of Progress:

USAID's Child Survival and Maternal Health Program," http://www
.usaid.gov/our_work/global_health/mch/ch/publications/csrept1.pdf.

4. International Monetary Fund and International Development
Association, "Heavily Indebted Poor Countries Initiative —
Statistical Update (2006)," 28, http://siteresources.worldbank.org/
INTDEBTDEPT/ProgressReports/20953987/032106.pdf.

5. Lauren Etter and Greg Hitt, "Farm Lobby Beats Back Assault
on Subsidies," *Wall Street Journal*, March 27, 2008, http://online.wsj
.com/article/SB120657645419967077.html.

Chapter 7: Hopeful Developments in U.S. Politics

1. John Nichols, "Remembering Molly Ivins," *The Nation*, January
21, 2007.

2. Alliance to End Hunger, "Hunger Message Project," http://
www.alliancetoendhunger.org/resources/.

3. Tom Freedman, *American Media Coverage of Africa* (Washington,
DC: Freedman Consulting, 2006).

4. "Letter from Bill and Melinda Gates," 2009, http://www
.gatesfoundation.org/about/Pages/bill-melinda-gates-letter.aspx.

5. Richard Stearns, *The Hole in Our Gospel* (Nashville: Thomas
Nelson, 2009), 196.

6. The U.S. President's Emergency Plan for AIDS Relief,
World AIDS Day 2009: Latest PEPFAR Results, http://www.pepfar.gov/
documents/organization/133033.pdf.

7. Sarah Turner and David Beckmann, *How U.S. Churches and
Society Are Responding to Increased Poverty* (Washington, DC: Bread for
the World, January 2010).

8. S. Bloomfield, "Popular in Africa: Bush Has Given More Aid
Than Any Other US President," *Independent*, February 17, 2008,
http://www.independent.co.uk/news/world/africa/popular-in-africa-
bush-has-given-more-aid-than-any-other-us-president-783387.html.

9. Tom Freedman, Sam Gill, Sam Feder, John Bridgeland, and
Meredith Copley, "The Issue of Poverty in the 2008 Campaign —
A Study of Print Media," 2008, http://www.naktv.net/Spotlight/
SpotlightMediaStudy.pdf.

Chapter 8: A Time to Change History for Hungry People

1. As of March 2010. See http://feedingamerica.org.

2. Center on Budget and Policy Priorities, "The Earned Income Tax Credit," December 4, 2009, http://www.cbpp.org/files/policybasics-eitc.pdf.

3. Intergovernmental Panel on Climate Change, "Climate Change 2007: Synthesis Report," November 2007, http://www.ipcc.ch/pdf/assessment-report/ar4/syr/ar4_syr_spm.pdf.

4. Organization for Economic Cooperation and Development, cited in InterAction, "The Other Partner: NGOs and Private Sector Funding for International Development & Relief," February 2009, 6.

5. World Bank, *World Development Report 2010: Development and Climate Change* (Washington, DC: World Bank, 2010).

6. Dennis Cauchon, "Tax Bills in 2009 at Lowest Level Since 1950," *USA Today*, May 11, 2010, http://www.usatoday.com/money/perfi/taxes/2010-05-10-taxes_N.htm. See also Gerald Prante, "A Closer Look at Popular USA Today Article Claiming Historically Low Taxes," Tax Foundation Tax Policy Blog, May 11, 2010, http://www.taxfoundation.org/blog/show/26292.html.

7. Center on Budget and Policy Priorities, "Where Do Our Federal Tax Dollars Go?" 2009, http://www.cbpp.org/cms/index.cfm?fa+view&id=1258.

Chapter 10: Take a Step

1. Robert Putnam and David Campbell, *American Grace: How Religion Is Reshaping Our Civic and Political Lives* (forthcoming), discussed in "Congregants Make Better Citizens," *Christian Century*, June 16, 2009, 16.

2. Richard Stearns, *The Hole in Our Gospel* (Nashville: Thomas Nelson, 2009), 217.

3. John Robbins, *The Food Revolution: How Your Diet Can Help Save Your Life and Our World* (San Francisco: Conari Press, 2001).

4. Jeffry Odell Korgen, *My Lord and My God: Engaging Catholics in Social Ministry* (Mahwah, NJ: Paulist Press, 2006).

5. The Association of Americans Resident Overseas, "5.25 Million Americans (Excluding Military) Live in 160-plus Countries," http://aaro.org/index.php?option=com_content&view=article&id=6&catid=4&Itemid=6. Also, U.S. Department of Commerce, "2008 United States Resident Travel Abroad," 2009, http://tinet.ita.doc.gov/outreachpages/download_data_table/2008_US_Travel_Abroad.pdf.

6. New York: Nation Books, 2009.

7. Jacqueline L. Salmon, "Churches Retool Mission Trips," *Washington Post*, July 5, 2008.

8. Richard A. Hoehn, *Up from Apathy* (Nashville: Abingdon Press, 1983).

INDEX